GUIDE

TO THE

Franciscan Monastery

WASHINGTON, D. C.

Guide

TO THE

Franciscan Monastery

WASHINGTON, D. C.

✠

A PILGRIMAGE TO
"The Holy Land of America"

WILDSIDE PRESS

TOGETHER WITH MANY INTERESTING FACTS
ABOUT THE ORDER OF ST. FRANCIS AND ITS
WORK IN THE HOLY LAND AND AMERICA

First Edition, 1898
Second Edition, 1900
Third Edition, 1914
Fourth Edition, 1929
Fifth Edition, 1934

Contents

	PAGE
Introduction	8
The Beginning	11
The Coming of the Friars	15
The Dedication	16
The Consecration	19
The Rosary Portico	23
A Rosary in Stone	29
The Monastery	33
The Holy Sepulchre	37
The Altar of Thabor	43
The Stone of Anointing	46
The Center Altar	47
The Altar of Calvary	51
The Chapel of St. Joseph	55
The Chapel of St. Francis	57
The Chapel of Penance	61
The Altar of the Holy Ghost	65
The Lady Chapel	67
The Chapel of St. Anthony	71
The Sacred Heart Altar	73
The Statues	75
The Votive Lamps	77
The Grotto of Nazareth	79
The Catacombs	83
The Martyr's Crypt	85
The Purgatory Chapel	89

	PAGE
The Catacomb Chapels	93
The Grotto of Bethlehem	95
The Valley and Grotto of Gethsemane	99
The Tomb of the Blessed Virgin	103
The Grotto of Lourdes	107
House of the Holy Family and Chapel of St. Anne	109
Way of the Cross	113
Chapel of the Ascension	117
The Portiuncula Chapel	119
The Monastery Cloister	121
The Purpose of the Monastery	126
The Franciscans and the World	128
The Franciscans and the Church	135
The Franciscans and America	141
The Franciscans and the Holy Land	147
Devotions Founded by the Franciscans	151
The Religious Life	157

GUIDE
TO THE
FRANCISCAN MONASTERY
WASHINGTON, D. C.

Introduction

THE cordial reception given by the public to the previous editions of the GUIDE TO THE FRANCISCAN MONASTERY encourages us to continue this labor of love. It is but natural that the interest awakened in the hearts of the hundreds of thousands who look for the first time on these reproductions of the Holy Shrines of Palestine should prompt the desire to acquire some remembrance of the Monastery.

This new edition has, besides the above, other reasons for its appearance. The various changes, both within and without the Monastery, have necessitated a revision of the Guide Book to include the improvements made since the foundation of Mount St. Sepulchre more than a third of a century ago.

To the devotion of countless souls in many lands who have given their mite that this Temple be erected to God's greater honor and glory, this beautiful Church stands as an eloquent and a lasting monument. So, too, its interior beauty is due to the generosity of numerous Benefactors who have donated Shrines, Altars, and ornaments to the service of God. That He may bless and keep them all, and be their "reward exceeding great," is our humble and constant prayer.

And in thanking God for the innumerable benefits received at His hands, we renew our trust in His Divine Providence for the future. We again pledge to Him our loyal efforts to spread a knowledge and love for the Holy Land and for the Sacred Places there, which He sanctified by His Life upon earth—those Shrines which Holy Mother Church has always venerated as her most precious heritage, applying to herself the words of Holy Scripture: "If I forget thee, O Jerusalem, let my right hand be forgotten!" (*Psalm cxxxvi, 5.*)

THE COMMISSARIAT OF THE HOLY LAND

The Beginning

"And I said, now have I begun: this is the change of the right hand of the Most High." (Psalm lxxvi, 11.)

ON a wooded eminence in the Nation's magnificent Capital, not far from the Catholic University of America, and overlooking the attractive suburb of Brookland, the Franciscan Monastery Memorial Church of the Holy Land rises in simple and solitary grandeur. The beautiful location is ideal because of its quiet seclusion, and its easy accessibility from the city. Following the example of Franciscan tradition, the Friars selected a hill for the site of their Monastery, naming it MOUNT SAINT SEPULCHRE, in honor of the Holy Sepulchre in Jerusalem, here reproduced as its characteristic and chief Shrine.

Years ago no visitor would have considered it worth while to wend his way toward this secluded spot, which then contained the deserted home of the McCeeney family. During the first half of the last century, the place was well cultivated and prosperous. But later on, years of neglect wrought their destructive work, leaving the old estate in a desolate condition. The beautiful trees had fallen prey to the axe of the vandal, the well-cultivated orchard had disappeared, and the fields had almost returned to their wild, primitive state.

It was in its forlorn and forsaken aspect of 1897 that one day in August a stranger visited the old estate. Despite its neglected appearance, he did not fail to see the rich possibilities that lay before him. The isolated position on a hill, and the varied nature of the grounds, the grove on the one hand and the slope on the other,

Left: "IN THE NATION'S MAGNIFICENT CAPITAL"

the fertile lowlands; all this framed by a view of unsurpassed beauty, so aroused his admiration that with the Psalmist he exclaimed: "This is my rest forever and ever; here will I dwell for I have chosen it." (*Psalm cxxxi*, 14.)

Before his mind arose a wonderful vision which was soon to become a reality. During his sojourn in the Holy Land he had conceived the idea of transplanting, as it were, into the New World the chief sanctuaries of our Redemption, where those who might not have the happiness of visiting Palestine could view them in facsimile.

No place seemed better adapted for the realization of this project and more fit for a Monastery than this ideal spot, where, away from the world, the hearts of its dwellers could send forth an incense of continual prayer.

Retracing his steps, the stranger left the lonely hill. But this was not the end. Months later the people of Washington were surprised by the news of the sale of the old McCeeney estate,* and rumor had it that it was to become the home of a Religious Community.

Meanwhile the Holy See had sanctioned the transfer of the Commissariat of the Holy Land from New York City, and His Eminence Cardinal Gibbons had graciously received the Franciscans into his archdiocese. The Catholic University extended a cordial welcome to this new affiliation, to be one of the pioneer Religious Communities forming the nucleus of what in later years has become a commonwealth of Religious houses, like those surrounding Oxford and Cambridge at the height of their academic glory.

---

*Note: The following sequence of former owners of the estate, going back through three centuries to the British Crown, may be of interest, particularly in connection with the Tercentenary celebra-

Then it became definitely known that the Franciscan Order had acquired the lovely spot on the mount, and a few Brothers were sent from the Commissariat of the Holy Land in New York to make such improvements on the grounds as the future needs of the institution would warrant.

---

tion of the Catholic colonization of Maryland, "sanctuary of religious tolerance":

Commissariat of the Holy Land, acquired by deed in 1897;
George E. Hamilton, by administrator's deed, 1889;
Harriet A. McCeeney, by bequest, 1870;
Edgar Patterson, by bequest, 1867;
Robert S. Patterson, by deed, 1845;
Elbert G. Emack, by deed, 1842;
Perez (Peris) Packard, by deed, 1836;
Alexander Young and others, by bequest;
Jasper M. Jackson, 1790, by bequest. (*In this year the District of Columbia was established*);
Jasper Mordint (variously Merdit, Manduit, and Manduitt);
William Jones, 1770, by Patent. (*During his ownership, Maryland by her Declaration of Independence of July 3, 1776, became one of the new Thirteen States*);
Frederick Calvert, 6th and last Lord Baltimore, 1751, by succession;
Charles Calvert, 5th Lord Baltimore, 1715, by succession;
Benedict Leonard Calvert, 4th Lord Baltimore, same year, by succession;
Charles Calvert, 3rd Lord Baltimore, 1675, by succession;
Cecil Calvert, 2nd Lord Baltimore, 1632, by Royal Patent. (*On March 25, 1634, the Feast of the Annunciation, the first Maryland colonists landed and attended at Mass on St. Clement's Island in Chesapeak Bay*);
Sir George Calvert, 1st Lord Baltimore, by Royal Grant in the same year from Charles I, ill-fated King of England.

The Coming of the Friars

"This is my rest forever and ever; here will I dwell for I have chosen it." (Psalm cxxxi, 14.)

LIKE all true pioneers, the little colony of Friars had to suffer many hardships. They were alone and strangers, poorly supplied with the barest necessities of life, yet they turned eagerly to their task. They divided their time between earnest prayer and hard work. Early in the morning they would trudge through the snow in the face of icy blasts, that they might assist at or serve the first Mass in the little village church.

Under their steadfast toil the desolate aspect of the grounds soon passed, and in its place garden and vineyard and orchard appeared. Briers gave way to the onslaught of the plow, and tilled fields sprang up in the wilderness. A view from the hill in the spring of 1899 showed a panorama of carefully arranged fields, cultivated and well cared for, framed by paths and byways lined with young trees.

Early in February of 1898 ground was broken for the new building which today crowns the hilltop, and the corner-stone was laid on the Feast of St. Joseph, March 19, of the same year. From the very beginning, the building of the Monastery aroused great interest in the city of Washington, and some of the wildest rumors gained circulation in the newspapers. The outlines of the foundation showed a plan of quite unusual shape, so that the numerous visitors were puzzled as to the meaning of this novel structure. But time passed on, the builders labored, and slowly and impressively rose the walls of the Monastery.

Left: AERIAL VIEW
OF THE MONASTERY

The Dedication

"The Most High has sanctified His own tabernacle."
(Psalm xlv, 5.)

THE Feast of the Stigmata of St. Francis, September 17, 1899, saw the dedication of the Church and Monastery. Clear and calm, the dawning woke into a most beautiful day whose very air seemed to breathe the spirit of the occasion. The solemn exercises of the dedication began at 10 o'clock, when the procession formed and passed around the Church and the cloister of the Monastery, which was blessed by Cardinal Gibbons, attended by numerous other Prelates and visiting priests. Through the Monastery and into the Church the procession passed, solemnly dedicating the edifice to the service of the Most High.

At the beginning of the Solemn Pontifical Mass the large Church was thronged, and great crowds gathered about the doorways. Archbishop Martinelli, later elevated to the Cardinalate and then Apostolic Delegate, was the celebrant, occupying a throne draped with the Papal white and gold on the Epistle side of the Church. Opposite was His Eminence Cardinal Gibbons on a throne of crimson. The other officers of the Mass were priests prominent in Catholic life in this country at that time.

A choir of sixty male voices sang the deep, soul-reaching tones of Gounod's Second Mass. The Very Rev. L. F. Kearney, Provincial of the Dominicans, delivered an eloquent sermon, carrying out the tradition by which the Dominicans have often been represented at Franciscan celebrations, in token of the friendship and sympathy between the founders of the two Orders.

A host of Knights of Columbus, who had taken charge of the occasion, were present at the services. They included more than one thousand from Washington, and several hundred from near-by cities. In the afternoon, after the Solemn Vespers, the Knights, amid the cheers of a multitude, raised two flags in front of the Church—the Stars and Stripes and the Cross of the Holy Land—thus in a sense pledging the United States to the work of redeeming the Sacred Places. Speeches were made, dwelling on the work of the Franciscans in America, and prophesying glorious achievements for the future. Throughout the day until dusk, crowds continued to pour into the Church, so that it is estimated that at least ten thousand entered its doors on the day of the Dedication.

And then the joyous ceremonies, the pomp and splendor of the day completed, the crimson rays of the setting sun gilded tower and cross, roof and dome, and the peaceful quiet of the twilight gave way to the more peaceful quiet of the moonlit night. Stillness lay upon the land as a benediction. It was as if the blessing of St. Francis himself had been fulfilled:

"*May He turn His countenance towards thee and give thee peace.*"

The Consecration

"The altar of holocaust and all its vessels . . . thou shalt consecrate." (Exodus xl, 10-11.)

HE twenty-fifth anniversary of the Dedication of the Monastery witnessed its solemn Consecration to the Most High God, the day chosen for the great event being once again the Feast of the Stigmata of St. Francis, September 17, 1924.

It was our happy privilege that the consecrating Prelate should be one of our own confrères, the late and everywhere-beloved Archbishop Albert T. Daeger, O.F.M., of Santa Fe, New Mexico, who was delegated for this important function by the Most Rev. Archbishop Curley of Baltimore.

The quarter of a century thus marked had been an eventful one, and looking back in retrospect, one beheld many a sacred event in our Church. The years had witnessed the investiture of young men with the Habit of St. Francis; they had seen them as they pronounced their Solemn Vows; young Levites had received at its Altar the sacred character of the Priesthood; they were the sorrowful witnesses, too, of the passing of members of the Mount's Community.

Amid all the eventful happenings of those years, two perhaps stand out with a greater brilliance. His Eminence Cardinal Gibbons selected our Church as the scene of the solemn commemoration of his Jubilee, celebrated on February 20, 1919, twenty years after he had officiated at the Dedication. The occasion was one of unique significance, marking as it did the aged Prince's observance of his fiftieth anniversary as

THE FOUNDER AND HIS WORK

Bishop, and the twenty-fifth as Cardinal. Present on that day were a Papal Legate, three Cardinals, the Apostolic Delegate, and a large number of Archbishops, Bishops, and other Prelates, making the scene one of a sacred splendor difficult to picture.

Outstanding, too, in the annals of the Mount was the Consecration of the Most Rev. William Turner as Bishop of Buffalo, N. Y., on March 10, 1919. Ever finding a true Franciscan welcome here during his years as Professor at the near-by Catholic University, the newly appointed Bishop chose our Church for his elevation to the episcopate, at the hands of Cardinal Gibbons. One of the co-consecrators then was Bishop Curley of St. Augustine, Fla., now successor to the Cardinal as Archbishop of Baltimore.

In the majestic and beautiful liturgy of the Catholic Church, there is perhaps no ceremony more impressive than the ancient rite whereby a Church is consecrated to the service of the Almighty. It was indeed inspiring, on the long anticipated day of Consecration, to behold the mitered Archbishop, surrounded by vested ministers and clergy, as he blessed and anointed with Holy Chrism the Monastery walls, and sealed relics of the Roman Martyrs Saints Christopher and Aurelia within its Altars. Consecrated with the Church edifice were five Altars, namely: the Center Altar dedicated to the Holy Trinity, and those commemorative of the Blessed Virgin, St. Joseph, St. Francis, and St. Anthony. Concluding the solemn rite, Pontifical Mass was offered at the newly consecrated Center Altar.

Thus was celebrated the great day which marked a quarter of a century of blessed service of God. It was a day which saw the fulfillment of a dream of uncounted years in the life of the venerable founder of the Monastery, Father Godfrey Schilling—that

"Stranger" whom the reader meets in the chapter called "The Beginning" within these pages.

A day which dawned with lowering skies changed to a happier mood as the sacred ceremonies were solemnized. And once again the golden rays of sunset mellowed into twilight, as they caressed two flags proudly floating in the breeze from their lofty standards—the glorious Stars and Stripes, and the Red and White of the Holy Land.

The Rosary Portico

"Go ye into His gates with praise, into His courts with hymns: and give glory to Him." (Psalm xcix, 4.)

AS THE visitor passes the Monastery Pilgrimage Hall, reminiscent of the early California Franciscan Missions, and wends his way to the top of the hill crowned by the Monastery, he is attracted to the graceful Rosary Portico which now meets his view. Entering this cloister-like enclosure through a noble arched gateway, he finds himself suddenly separated from a busy world and standing—perhaps for the first time—within the sacred precincts of a Monastery. For the moment, the Portico has become for him a veritable Cloister, and a feeling of peace and tranquillity steals over him, as his admiring gaze rests upon the majestic Church, surrounded by well-kept lawns and gardens.

Before him stands an heroic statue of St. Christopher, the patron of travelers, bearing the precious burden of the Christ Child. At the left is a bronze statue representing St. Francis of Assisi begging a little boy not to sell into captivity some doves which he holds. The story here immortalized relates that this great lover of Nature and Nature's God was given the doves, which he freed, bidding them return to the element which their Creator had provided for them. Hidden partly by the Church and trees, at the left is seen a small Chapel built of rough-hewn stones. It is the Chapel of Our Lady of the Angels, or Portiuncula.

Meanwhile, impressed by the beauty of the sur-

The Monastery Pilgrimage Hall

roundings, the visitor turns his attention to the Portico, whose arches and vari-tinted columns cannot but evoke the admiration of the beholder. Pausing to read an inscription at the entrance, he learns that fifteen of the Chapels of the Portico commemorate in bas-relief panels the Fifteen Mysteries of the Rosary, namely: the Five Joyful Mysteries of the Annunciation, the Visitation, the Birth of Our Saviour, the Presentation, the Finding of the Child Jesus in the Temple; the Sorrowful Mysteries of the Agony in the Garden, the Scourging at the Pillar, the Crowning with Thorns, Jesus Carrying His Cross, the Crucifixion; and the Glorious Mysteries of the Resurrection, the Ascension, the Descent of the Holy Ghost upon the Apostles, the Assumption, and the Coronation of the Blessed Virgin in Heaven. To these have been added two other Chapels in commemoration of the Founding of the Third Order of St. Francis and the Institution of the Franciscan Rosary of the Seven Joys.

The architectural lines of the structure take on a new significance, when it is learned that the ten arches between the Chapels symbolize the ten *Hail Marys* of the decades of the Rosary. In the spandrels above the columns are reproduced in colored mosaic religious emblems, many of which have their origin in Christian antiquity.

Above the massive double gateway of the Portico is the inscription, "Hosanna to the Son of David. Blessed is he that cometh in the name of the Lord"; while at its top a Cross proclaims the sanctity of the place to which it is the entrance. In a niche between the arches of the gate, a Statue of St. Bernardine of Siena, a fifteenth century Franciscan whose missionary life was devoted to promoting reverence to the Holy Name of Jesus, seems to bid the visitor "Welcome."

On the inner side is a statue representing St. Michael, the Archangel, celestial defender of the Church.

The gently sloping tiled roof of the Portico, the harmonious color-scheme of the entire structure, surrounded by myriads of roses in keeping with its title, Portico of the Rosary, have attracted nation-wide admiration, like the Monastery of which it is a part. It was solemnly blessed on Rosary Sunday, October 3, 1926, a quarter of a century after the building of the Church itself.

Left: WITHIN THE
PORTICO GATEWAY

A Rosary in Stone

Hail, Mary, full of grace, the Lord is with thee; blessed art thou among women,* and blessed is the fruit of thy womb,† Jesus. Holy Mary, Mother of God,‡ pray for us sinners now and at the hour of our death. Amen. (St. Luke i, *28, †42, ‡43.)

ENSHRINED within the hallowed Chapels of the Rosary Portico are Memorial Panels, inscribed with the inspired words of the Apostles' Creed, the Lord's Prayer, and the Hail Mary or *Ave Maria*.

As the Rosary itself, beginning with the Sign of the Cross and the Apostles' Creed, consists of fifteen decades or groups of ten *Ave Marias* preceded by the Lord's Prayer, so the Rosary Portico carries out this sacred theme in its Chapels dedicated to the Fifteen Mysteries of the Rosary, united to one another by decades of arches. The sublime prayers comprising that Rosary are here immortalized in artistic and enduring Tablets of colored ceramics, donated by various generous benefactors. Because of the importance of this unique undertaking, this "Rosary in Stone" has been perpetuated in a book which is in keeping with the ideals that have inspired this entire labor of love.

The words uttered by the Angel to the Immaculate Mother of Jesus, of whom the Gospel prophesies "All generations shall call me blessed" (St. *Luke i, 48*), have re-echoed down the ages and over the world, inspiring great composers, painters, sculptors, and poets of every century. It is this Angelic *Ave* which the pilgrim finds here in the languages of "nations, and tribes, and peoples, and tongues."

This beautiful prayer—begun by an Angel of

Left: ALONG THE ROSARY PORTICO

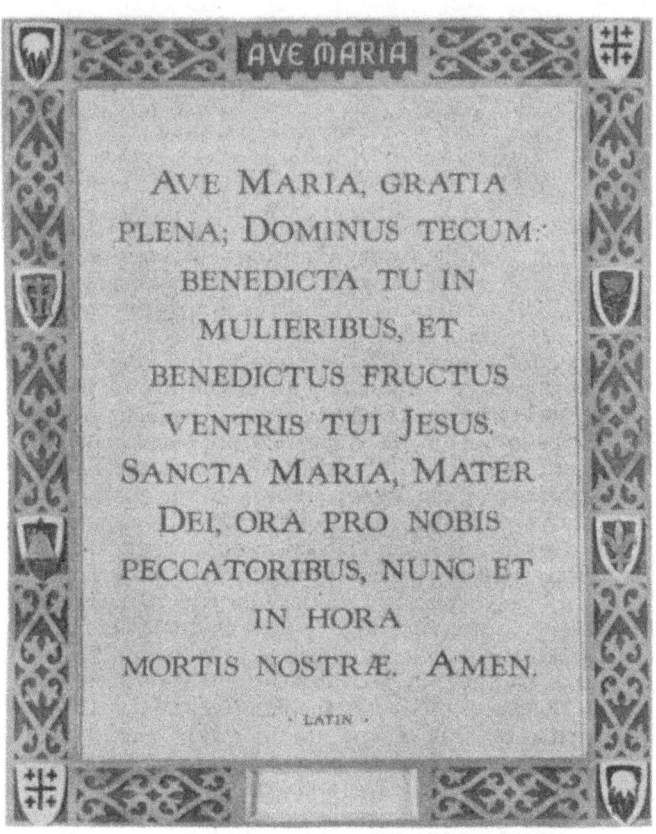

The Latin Ave Maria Tablet

Heaven and concluded by sin-laden man—is translated into one hundred fifty languages. The forgotten tongues of ancient Assyria and Egypt live once again; one sees the strange Oriental characters of Ethiopia, Arabia, and mystic lands of the East; Latin and Greek and Hebrew, used in the Liturgy of the Mass today, are mingled with the strange vernaculars of the South Sea Isles and the tribes of Africa. Through the centuries our own English mother-tongue is traced back to the Anglo-Saxon, and to the even older Gothic, from which it sprang. The fast disappearing languages of the aboriginal Indian Tribes of America are recorded for posterity in these Memorials, sacred to the Maid of Nazareth, whom the poet Wordsworth called "Our tainted nature's solitary boast."

The Monastery

"And they shall make me a sanctuary, and I will dwell in the midst of them." (Exodus xxv, 8.)

ENTERING the Sacristy or Vestry (No. 1 on the plan of the Church on page 34), and passing through the Chapel of St. Joseph, the Pilgrim-visitor finds himself within the Monastery Church.

Since Mount Saint Sepulchre was opened to the public, this unique Memorial Church of the Holy Land has attracted numberless visitors, and a continuous stream of pilgrims flows through its portals to view the sacred edifice, so beautiful in its simplicity, and the Holy Shrines there reproduced with faithful exactitude.

The general architectural outlines of the Church are Byzantine, with a slight trend toward the Italian Renaissance, so that the artistic effects of the great Hagia Sophia in Constantinople and of the beautiful Certosa of Pavia have been adapted to Franciscan simplicity. The Church follows the lines of the Five-fold Cross, which formed the coat-of-arms of the Latin Kingdom of Jerusalem, the large cross constituting the main body of the Church, and the small ones the Chapels. This emblem is reproduced in the pavement of the Church in Venetian mosaic, so that the whole structure resting thereon declares the purpose of the institution itself, being dedicated to the service and welfare of the Holy Land. This cross, which appears again and again in Mount Saint Sepulchre, is symbolic of the Five Wounds of Our Lord. It greets the pilgrim from the lofty gable of the Church, and is never absent from his sight during his visit.

Left: THE CHURCH

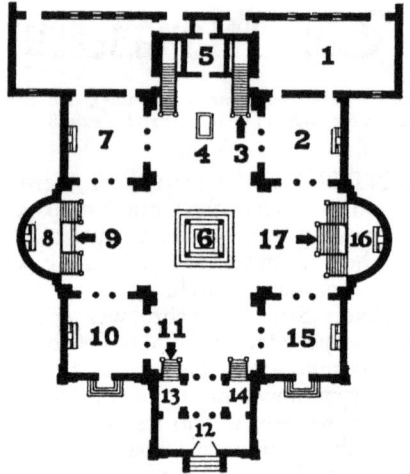

Plan of the Church

1 · Sacristy.
2 · Chapel of St. Joseph.
3 · Stairs to Altar of Thabor.
4 · Stone of the Anointing.
5 · The Holy Sepulchre.
6 · Center Altar.
7 · Chapel of St. Francis.
8 · Altar of the Holy Ghost.
9 · Exit from Grotto of Bethlehem.
10 · Chapel of the Blessed Virgin.
11 · Stairs to Altar of Calvary.
12 · Main Entrance.
13 · Chapel of the Crowning with Thorns.
14 · Chapel of the Scourging.
15 · Chapel of St. Anthony.
16 · Altar of the Sacred Heart.
17 · Entrance to Grottoes.

The architectural theme is principally evident in the entrances to the four chapels. This triple arch serves as a base for a series of four upper arches, which in turn support the high arched windows of the clerestory, the whole arrangement of rows of graceful columns and ascending arches of various sizes forming a striking effect. The ceiling, partly vaulted and partly flat, is ornamented with panels and rosettes. The architect of the Church and Monastery was the well-known Aristides Leonori, a member of the Third Order of St. Francis, who died in Rome in 1928, renowned for sanctity of life and charity for the poor.

The light in the Church is agreeably tempered by beautiful stained-glass windows, in nearly all of which are represented Saints of the Three Orders of St. Francis, who seem to step out of their frames to welcome the visitor, inviting him to prayer and meditation. These are the figures of holy men and women of the last seven centuries, renowned for learning, apostolic zeal, piety, and works of charity, who gave their lives to God and followed Our Lord on the narrow path of the evangelical counsels in the Order of St. Francis of Assisi. When the evening sun sends its golden rays into the Church, these resplendent forms shine with a wonderful brightness which seems to reflect the eternal bliss of the Saints. The world may have ridiculed them for their piety and austere life, but it will one day say: "These are they, whom we had some time in derision, and for a parable of reproach. We fools esteemed their life madness, and their end without honor. Behold, now they are numbered among the children of God, and their lot is among the Saints." (*Wisdom v, 3-5.*)

The Holy See has conceded the Indulgences of the Holy Places of Palestine to these reproductions, designated respectively by bronze Crosses. A plenary Indulgence may be gained at each by the recitation of one *Our Father* and *Hail Mary*, subject to the condition that one is in a state of grace, or free from the guilt of mortal sin.*

Upon entering the Church, the gaze of the visitor is drawn instinctively to three Shrines, the majesty and beauty of which command rapt attention. At the right is the elevated Sanctuary of Mount Thabor, with its Altar of the Blessed Sacrament surrounded by a glorious relief-panel depicting the Transfiguration of Our Divine Lord. Between the marble stairways leading up to this Sanctuary is a faithful copy of the Holy Sepulchre in Jerusalem, for which the Monastery was named MOUNT SAINT SEPULCHRE, or the Mount of the Holy Sepulchre.

In the center of the Church beneath the lofty dome stands the Center Altar, inspiring in its simple and magnificent lines. Beyond this stately canopied Altar, attention is held by the realistic representation of the Crucifixion, which characterizes the Sanctuary of Calvary in the west nave.

---

*Indulgences are not the remission of sins, but of the punishment due to sins after their forgiveness in the Sacrament of Penance, or Confession. The Indulgenced Shrines here are: the Holy Sepulchre, Stone of Anointing, Altar of Calvary, Grotto of Nazareth, Altar of the Nativity, the Manger, Altar of the Magi, Grotto of Gethsemane, Tomb of the Blessed Virgin, and the Chapel of the Ascension.

The Holy Sepulchre

"His Sepulchre shall be glorious." (Isaias xi, 10.)

THE Sepulchre of Jesus Christ has been the center of devotion to Christians in every age and clime. The Crusaders freely shed their blood for its recovery, and throughout the Middle Ages resounded the words: "God help us and the Holy Sepulchre." Such a religious veneration for this holy spot is inspired by the fact that the Resurrection of Christ is the confirmation of His doctrine, so much so that St. Paul did not hesitate to say: "If Christ be not risen again, then is our preaching in vain and your faith is also vain." (*I Cor. xv*, 14.)

The Holy Sepulchre is the tomb which the noble Joseph of Arimathea had prepared for himself in a garden outside the city walls of that period, and but a stone's throw from Calvary. According to the Jewish custom, the noble Israelite had caused it to be cut into rock, so as to provide a bench for the reception of a body. It was on this that Christ's Sacred Body was laid when taken down from the Cross. The Tomb had the customary ante-chamber, now called the Chapel of the Angel, because it was there that the Angel announced to the holy women the Saviour's Resurrection.

In her holy fervor to erect a magnificent temple over so sacred a spot, St. Helena, the mother of Constantine, about 325 A.D., cut away the hillside, leaving only the Tomb itself intact, and over this she built a beautiful chapel, which was called the *Anastasis* or Resurrection. Since then, the Holy Sepulchre has passed through many vicissitudes, and the present chapel was erected

ORIGINAL FORM OF THE HOLY SEPULCHRE
1. ANTE-CHAMBER;   2. BURIAL CHAMBER;   3. REVOLVING STONE

over the Sacred Tomb by the Greeks after a fire in 1809. In Jerusalem the Holy Sepulchre stands in the center of the 4th century Basilica rotunda, surrounded by arched galleries and surmounted by a dome. In our Church, however, the facsimile reproduction of the Holy Sepulchre has been placed in the eastern nave, where it is a copy, in other respects, of the one in Jerusalem as it exists today.

A pilgrimage to the Holy Sepulchre has ever been regarded by Christians as a great privilege and their feeling finds expression in the inspiring words of St. Bernard: "How sweet it is to pilgrims, after a long and wearisome journey, after many dangers by land and sea, finally to rest where they know their Lord has rested!"

Even as one beholds the Holy Sepulchre in Jerusalem, so dear to the heart of every Catholic, so the pilgrim to Mount Saint Sepulchre is brought face to face, as

Left: THE HOLY SEPULCHRE
AND STONE OF ANOINTING

PRESENT FORM OF THE HOLY SEPULCHRE
1. CHAPEL OF THE ANGEL (ANTE-CHAMBER); 2. BURIAL CHAMBER

though time and space are annihilated, with the place where the Lord was laid. A minute ago he stood at the doorway and gazed at the distant hills, and the far-reaching fields of America. A step, and the New World is forgotten—for surely this place, whose very air breathes a holy calm and peace, can have nothing in common with the busy realms of commerce and the noisy marts of trade, so recently left behind.

Through a low door one enters the outer room of the Tomb. Here in the center, supported by a pedestal, is a stone called the STONE OF THE ANGEL, the original of which tradition says is a fragment of the very stone from which the Angelic Messenger of Heaven announced the glad tidings of the Resurrection on that glorious Easter morning nineteen hundred years ago. The copy here contains a stone from Jerusalem.

Beyond another door, lower even than the first, is the burial chamber, similar to the one where the body of Our Lord was laid on the First Good Friday. Memorial lamps hang before a bas-relief of Raphael's "Resurrection." The tabernacle here becomes the

Tomb of the Eucharistic Christ on each Holy Thursday and Good Friday, when this Shrine is used as the Holy Week Repository of the Blessed Sacrament. A touching figure of the Dead Christ reposes on the burial couch of this Holy Sepulchre. Otherwise the room is devoid of ornament, for here one does not seek beauty—the beauty of the spot is the beauty of holiness.

To protect from the touch of profane hands the place where the Sacred Body of Jesus reposed, a slab of marble was placed over it in the twelfth century. Knowing well the greed of the Turks, who would seize any stone of value, workmen cut a crevice in the slab, imitating a crack such as would have resulted had the marble been broken. The artifice served its purpose, and the marble remains in the Holy Sepulchre today, scarred as here seen.

Though this Shrine of the Holy Sepulchre is only a facsimile of the original, yet it is indeed holy ground, for here the Eucharistic Sacrifice is offered. And as the years come and go, countless pilgrims kneel here in prayer, inspired to more fervent faith by these striking reminders of the awful price of our Redemption. It overpowers, it fills the heart with divine love, and prayer rises to the lips as water from an overflowing fountain.

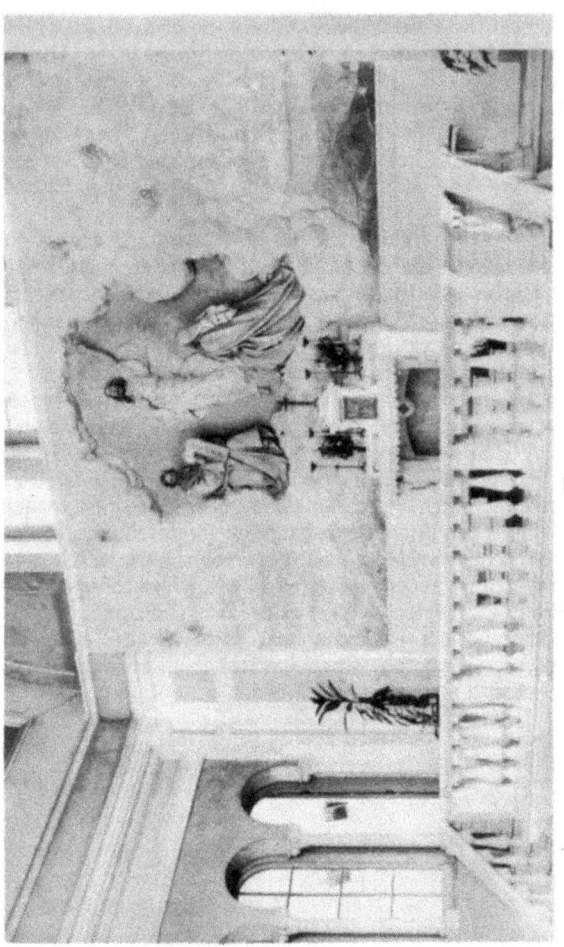

Altar of the Transfiguration

The Altar of Thabor

"He was transfigured before them."
(St. Matthew xvii, 2.)

ABOVE the Holy Sepulchre is the Altar of Thabor, commemorating the Transfiguration of Our Lord. In the midst of Galilee, Mount Thabor rises towards the sky like a mighty altar, from which the Lord on the day of the Transfiguration radiated His divine glory. It was like a heavenly Benediction, in which His resplendent Body shone out as from a celestial monstrance.

A panorama of wondrous beauty unfolds itself to the pilgrim visiting this privileged mountain. The snow-capped head of the Great Hermon rises to the north; the unbroken chain of the Hauran stretches to the east; the silvered waves of the Mediterranean sparkle in the west, while to the south extend the verdant plains and undulating hills of Samaria. The summit of Thabor is like an irregular platform, marked by the ruins of an extensive fortress and ancient churches. Here in the fourth century a Basilica was erected, and in the sixth mention is made of three churches on Mount Thabor. Later the Benedictines founded an Abbey there. These majestic ruins were visited in 1889 by the first Catholic Pilgrimage to the Holy Land from the United States. The memory of Our Lord's Transfiguration, the impressive remains of the ancient Basilica, and the beautiful scenes around them, made a lasting impression on the pilgrims from the New World, who in their enthusiasm declared their intention of rebuilding the ancient church on the spot where the Divinity of

Christ had been so wondrously set forth. The execution of that solemn pledge of the Catholics of this Republic to rebuild that Shrine of Christ's glory was long delayed by circumstances. But today there stands on the heights of Thabor a magnificent Basilica dedicated to the Saviour's Transfiguration. The re-erection of this ancient church was entrusted to the Catholics of America by Pope Benedict XV in 1919, the funds for the great undertaking being collected and transmitted to Palestine by this Commissariat. The completed temple was solemnly consecrated by a Cardinal Papal Legate in 1924.

To our own Altar of Thabor one ascends to receive Holy Communion, when, like the favored Apostles Peter, James, and John, the faithful are admitted to the intimate companionship of Jesus in the Blessed Sacrament to share, as it were, in their glorious vision, and to receive at that divine fountain encouragement and consolation amidst the trials of life.

Above the Altar is a beautiful panel of the Transfiguration, made after the conception of Doré. Surrounded by a great halo of clouds is seen the sublime figure of Our Lord, with Moses holding the Tables of the Law and Elias looking up to the Expected of the Nations in an adoring attitude. Angels appear in the sky, and in the scene below are the hills of Galilee and a glimpse of the Sea of Genesareth.

The Blessed Sacrament is reserved in this highest and most prominent part of the Church, because it is meet that the Lord, up to Whom all creatures must look, should reside as on a Throne of majesty. In a figurative sense this is the Cenacle, where the sanctuary lamp proclaims His continual presence and reminds us that it is His delight to be with the children of men.

High above the Altar a large window bears the representation of the Eternal Father enthroned in majesty, while below Him is the Dove of the Holy Spirit, overshadowing the Divine Son in His Transfiguration. It is as though we could hear the Creator's voice once again proclaim: "This is My beloved Son, in Whom I am well pleased; hear ye Him!" (*St. Matthew xvii, 5.*)

The Stone of Anointing

"They took, therefore, the body of Jesus and bound it in linen cloths, with the spices." (St. John xix, 40.)

BEFORE the Holy Sepulchre is seen a facsimile of the Stone of Unction, as it appears today in the Basilica of the Holy Sepulchre in Jerusalem. There it marks the place where the body of Jesus when taken down from the Cross, and in accordance with the Jewish funeral customs was anointed and wrapped in linen cloths for burial in the Tomb. The original Stone is covered by a flat monument of red marble, here reproduced.

During long centuries of strife and persecution, this sacred Shrine was always held in veneration, being covered with a beautiful mosaic as early as the time of St. Helena, in the fourth century. Thus it was when the Franciscans first assumed care of the Sacred Places of the Holy Land in the thirteenth century. Since a part of the primitive mosaic had been destroyed, the Friars replaced it with a slab of black marble. In 1808 this was carried away by the Greeks, who substituted the red stone found there today. This exact replica of the Shrine of the Saviour's Anointing is made of Palestine marble.

The Center Altar

"I will go in to the Altar of God." (Psalm xlii, 4.)

THE majestic Altar, dedicated to the Most Holy Trinity, forms the nucleus around which all the other Altars of the Church face as in silent adoration.

This square Altar, constructed of native white marble, is surmounted by a canopy supported by four columns, symbolical of the four Evangelists; from this canopy hang twelve lamps in honor of the Twelve Apostles. The whole structure is of a Byzantine style, harmonizing with the architecture of the Church.

At the Gospel side of the Altar is seen a Paschal Candlestick, artistically wrought in the form of a twisted marble column, inset with vari-colored mosaics, a copy of a very old one in the Church of St. Clement in Rome. Here the Paschal Candle burns at the principal services from Easter Saturday until after the chanting of the Gospel at the Solemn Mass on Ascension Thursday, symbolizing the forty days during which Our Lord dwelt upon earth after His Resurrection.

Near the Altar on the Gospel side is the Throne, made of white Italian marble, and inlaid with a profusion of colored and gold mosaics, porphyry, verde antique, and semi-precious marbles. The Throne, similar to ancient ones in Rome, is occupied whenever the Archbishop or a Cardinal assists pontifically in the Divine Services.

On the Epistle side opposite is the bench occupied by the Celebrant, Deacon, and Subdeacon during the chanting by the choir of the *Gloria* and *Credo* at Solemn

The Center Altar

High Mass. The marble table near by is for the Chalice, Book of the Gospels, etc., used at these services.

Mass is solemnized at this Altar on Sundays and Holy Days, and Benediction with the Most Blessed Sacrament is given here. It is an impressive sight to see the Eucharistic Lord borne down from Thabor to spend a little while among His faithful children, to receive their homage and to impart to them His divine blessing. Truly does this remind us of the words of Holy Scripture: "My delights were to be with the children of men." (*Proverbs viii*, 31.)

The Altar of Calvary

"That place which is called Calvary, where they crucified Him." (St. John xix, 17-18.)

THE most sacred spot in the whole world is the holy hill where the drama of the Crucifixion was enacted, of which the four Evangelists have left such graphic and touching recitals. Calvary, or Golgotha, was not a mountain, as is the general conception, but a rocky knoll, skull-shaped, and situated not far from the ancient wall of Jerusalem, whence the Crucifixion could be witnessed by the populace.

Tradition tells us that Our Lord, as He hung on the wood of shame, looked westward, where His Faith was to take the firmest hold on mankind. And, indeed, ever since the time of Christ, civilization has gone westward, until its beneficial rays lighted on America, where today the Church counts more than twenty millions of devoted children in the United States alone.

The height of Calvary here corresponds with the elevation of that holy place above the level of the Basilica which encloses it in Jerusalem, while the distance from the Holy Sepulchre is approximately the same as in the Holy City: thus Our Lord could view from His Cross the place destined for His sacred burial.

This Altar is a facsimile of the Greek altar in Jerusalem which covers the place where the Saviour of the world gave up His life for the redemption of mankind. The spot where the Cross stood is indicated by a disc below the Altar, and to the right is represented the rent in the rock, caused by the earthquake at Our Lord's death.

Left: THE CALVARY ALTAR
OF THE CRUCIFIXION

In back of our Altar of Cavalry is a magnificent relief panel representing the Crucifixion. This great panel, which fills the entire end of the nave, depicts in a realistic manner the tragedy of the First Good Friday. With a fidelity which betokens deep and religious feeling, the sculptor has shown Our Lord at that moment when, knowing that His earthly mission of Redemption is finished, He bows His thorn-crowned head, and uttering the terrifying words "*Consummatum est*—It is consummated," He dies. Close by the Cross stands the Virgin Mother, comforted by St. John the Beloved Disciple. The penitent Magdalen is seen at the foot of the Cross overcome with grief. At the Saviour's right, the penitent thief Dismas looks with profound gratitude toward Him Who has just promised Paradise to him. Nearby are seen the faithful disciples and the holy women in attitudes of grief, mingled with love and adoration.

As one looks to the opposite side of the picture, so strangely real, the scene changes. Instead of the faithful followers of the Messias, one beholds, overshadowed by the approaching darkness, the enemies of Jesus. Relieved only by the figure of Longinus the Centurion, on whom the light of Faith is just dawning, are the chiefs of the synagogue, the Pharisees, and the rabble, whose thirst for blood was proclaimed but a short time before by "Crucify Him! Crucify Him!" Hanging on his cross above them is the impenitent thief, whom tradition calls Gesmas, cursing and reviling Him Who could have saved him, even as Dismas, his companion. Below, almost repulsive in their coarseness, soldiers cast lots for the garments of the dying Redeemer, little heeding the oncoming gloom that foretells the awful revulsion whereby even inanimate Nature protested against the murder of the Divine Saviour.

Back of the Cross, its walls and ramparts majestically spread across the vast panel, while its domes and towers are bathed in the rays of a crimson sun, lies the deicide city of Jerusalem—the city whose fate crushed the heart of the Saviour, when once He sobbed out on Olivet's heights those words so full of love and tenderness: "Jerusalem, Jerusalem, thou that killest the prophets and stonest them that are sent unto thee! How often would I have gathered together thy children as the hen doth gather her chickens under her wings, and thou wouldst not!" Soon that proud and opulent city will be shaken to its very foundation, the cheerful rays of the sun, even now turning to a bloody hue, will darken and will disappear, striking nameless terror into the hearts of the inhabitants. Soon the sacred veil of the Temple will be rent and the Holy of Holies—no longer holy—will be exposed to the gaze of every passerby. Even now the smoke of the noonday sacrifice is seen to curl up hazily from the sanctuary, its thin cloud pale and ghastly—the last sacrifice of the Old Law: on Calvary nearby is taking place the First Sacrifice of the New Law.

Above the Crucifixion panel are three stained-glass windows. The one in the center represents St. Francis; at the left St. Louis, the Crusader-King; and to the right St. Helena, the mother of Constantine the Great and imperial benefactress of the Holy Places. From this sanctuary an impressive vista is to be had of the Main Altar and the Church in general.

Before leaving this holy place, let one kneel before the Altar and pray: "Look down, O Lord, upon us Thy people for whom Our Lord Jesus Christ vouchsafed to be delivered into the hands of wicked men, and to suffer the agony and death of the Cross, Who livest and reignest for ever and ever. Amen."

Altar of St. Joseph

The Chapel of St. Joseph

"*Joseph . . . a just man.*" (St. Matthew i, 19.)

EVERY Catholic Altar in the world is dedicated to Almighty God, sometimes in commemoration of a particular event, as the Transfiguration, or in memory of God's Saints. St. Joseph well deserves an Altar in the Memorial Church of the Holy Land, for his life and virtues, so intimately connected with those of Jesus and the Holy Family, are forever associated with the Holy Land. His praise is sung in Holy Scripture, where he is called a "just man," a title equivalent to canonization. And indeed must he have been such, since he was privileged to carry in his arms and to caress the Infant Jesus, and to protect the youth of Our Lord, Who was submissive to him, obeying him and working under his direction during the years of the tranquil, hidden life at Nazareth.

The death of St. Joseph, which is supposed to have occurred shortly before the public ministry of Christ, is represented by a painting on the wall at the Gospel side of the Altar. Tradition relates that he died in the arms of Jesus and Mary, for which reason he is invoked as the Patron of a holy death.

The veneration of St. Joseph is ancient, but his Feast was introduced into the Western Church only after the Crusades. The pilgrims venerated his memory at Bethlehem and Nazareth, and they brought to Europe the Office which was then recited by the Religious in the ancient monasteries of St. Sabas and Mount Carmel. The Franciscans were the first to adopt it and to sing the praises of the Foster-father of

Jesus in their churches. St. Bernardine, a follower of St. Francis, wrote a masterly and luminous treatise on the virtues and excellencies of St. Joseph, from which subsequent writers have drawn their inspiration.

The statue of St. Joseph, which adorns the Altar, represents the Saint holding the Infant Jesus in his arms. The two bas-relief panels represent the Espousal of St. Joseph and the Blessed Virgin, and the Flight of the Holy Family into Egypt.

The Chapel of St. Francis

"And He gave him commandments . . . and a law of life and instruction." (Ecclesiasticus xlv, 6.)

IN the beautiful plain of Umbria in Italy stands Assisi, famous as the birthplace of him who, because of his loving spirit, has been called "Sweet Saint Francis." The son of a rich merchant, he was eminent for his wealth, but more so for his constant and unflinching virtue.

A sudden flash of grace, which came to him as he lay sick near to death, turned his thoughts from the smiling vanities of the world to the deeper facts of eternity. Overcome by a hitherto unknown longing for a better world, the image of the Saviour became more real to his eyes, and he loved Him with an ever-deepening and more intense adoration.

One day when he listened to the words of Christ: "If thou wilt be perfect, go sell what thou hast and give to the poor, and thou wilt have treasure in heaven, and come follow Me," he stripped himself of his rich apparel and, garbed in the clothes of a poor man, he became a beggar in the midst of luxury. Neither scorn nor ridicule had power to turn him from the path he had chosen. Disowned and disinherited by his father, he bore all for the sake of his Master, in Whose steps he endeavored to follow.

Disciples were not slow in flocking to his side, and in 1209, with the approbation of the Holy See, he founded the Order of Friars Minor, in Latin called *Ordo Fratum Minorum,* or "Order of Lesser Brothers."*

---

* The initials "O.F.M.," written after the names of Franciscans, indicate membership in the Order of Friars Minor.

ALTAR OF ST. FRANCIS OF ASSISI

Three years later the Second Order had its beginning, when Clare, a noble lady of Assisi, bade farewell to the world and donned a coarse garb of penitence.

There were many who wished to join this fast-growing army of Saints, but worldly duties and responsibilities would not allow them. To this end the Third Order sprang up, spreading throughout Christendom. Kings and noblemen added to their honors and regal garb the humble robe of the Poor Man of Assisi. To the influence of the Third Order is credited the abolition of many of the baneful customs of mediaeval feudalism.

It was after his return from a pilgrimage to Palestine that the crowning glory of his life was conferred on St. Francis. At midnight on Mt. Alverna he chanted Matins with his Brethren as usual. Then he went out to a place where there was a large Crucifix among the trees. Kneeling before it, he meditated on the sufferings of Christ, for it was the eve of the Feast of the Exaltation of the Holy Cross. As he prayed his Saviour that he might participate in some degree in His sufferings, the heavens opened before him and from on high there appeared a Seraph as though crucified, on whom Francis beheld the marks of the Five Wounds. The Seraph was Our Saviour, and He spoke to Francis, and the heart of the Saint became transformed and the marks of the Wounds appeared on his own body. In his hands appeared nails which seemed to have grown from his flesh, and his side appeared as if pierced with a lance, and blood from the wound stained his habit.

This stigmatization was the seal, as it were, of God's acceptance of the work of his earthly life. The Church has established the truth of this great mystery and has formally instituted a Festival to commemorate it on

September 17, the date chosen for Dedication and Consecration of Mount Saint Sepulchre.

A number of distinguished non-Catholics look with veneration to St. Francis, and have written his life. Some have adopted the Rule of the Third Order, and several Anglican communities have even accepted his Rules of the First and Second Orders in all their severity. Paul Sabatier and other distinguished Protestants are renowned for their Franciscan studies, and the Salvation Army proposed our Seraphic Saint as a model to its members in the little booklet called "Brother Francis, or Less than the Least."

The two relief panels at the sides of the statue of St. Francis, after a painting by Murillo, represent him blessing St. Louis of France and St. Elizabeth of Hungary, Royal members and Patrons of the Third Order; and his receiving the Stigmata of the Five Wounds.

An artistic group of carved wood statuary on the right side of the Chapel represents the sorrowful meeting of Our Lord and His Blessed Mother on the way to Calvary.

The Chapel of Penance

"Whose sins you shall forgive, they are forgiven them." (St. John xx, 23.)

COMPASSION is the characteristic of a loving heart, and therefore we find near the Altar of every Catholic Church the confessional, which is the tribunal, not of punishment, but of forgiveness and mercy.

As in the Holy Eucharist Jesus has erected a throne of His undying love towards us, so the Sacrament of Penance is the throne of His mercy, where He extends His pardon to the weeping Peter and to the penitent Magdalen. Penance is the Sacrament of the compassion of Jesus, of contrition, of reparation, and amendment of life.

Cardinal Newman, writing of the love of Our Lord in this Sacrament, observes thus beautifully:

"The presence of Jesus in the Holy Eucharist is real and substantial, proper and personal, in all the fullness of His Godhead and manhood. His presence in the Sacrament of Penance is by representation and grace. In the Holy Eucharist Jesus manifests Himself in His royalty, power, and glory. In the Sacrament of Penance in His tenderness as a Physician and His compassion as the Good Shepherd. In the former, He attracts and transforms us chiefly by His divine attributes; in the latter, by His human experience, sympathy, and pity.

"In the Holy Eucharist Jesus draws us upwards to Himself; in the Sacrament of Penance He stoops down to listen to us and to open to us His Sacred Heart in the midst of our sins and in the hour of our greatest miseries. The Holy Eucharist is Jesus reigning amongst

Christ and the Repentant Sinner

[62]

the just; the Sacrament of Penance is Jesus seeking among sinners for those that are lost; the former is the Sacrament of Saints, the latter, of the sinful; and therefore to such as we are it comes down with a singular nearness, an intimate contact with our needs, and an articulate and human voice of help and solace.

"Therefore the Sacrament of Penance is loved by Catholics and hated by the world. Like the pillar which of old guided the people of God, to us it is all light; to the world it is all darkness. There are two things of which the world would fain rid itself—of the Day of Judgment and the Sacrament of Penance; of the former because it is searching and inevitable, of the latter because it is the anticipation and witness of judgment to come. For this cause, there is no evil that the world will not say of the Confessional. It would dethrone the Eternal Judge, if it could, therefore it spurns the judge who sits in the tribunal of penance, because he is within reach of its hand. And not only the world without the Church, but the world within its unity, the impure, the false, the proud, the lukewarm, the worldly Catholic, and in a word, all who are impenitent, both fear and shrink from the shadow of the Great White Throne which falls on them from the Sacrament of Penance."

Altar of the Holy Ghost

"The Holy Ghost, Whom the Father will send in My Name, He will teach you all things."
(St. John xiv, 26.)

THE descent of the Holy Ghost upon the Apostles has been rightly called the birthday of the Church. Gathered together in the Upper Room of the Cenacle in Jerusalem on Pentecost, fifty days after Easter, the faithful band of Apostles awaited in fear and trembling the coming of the Comforter promised by Christ. From that day, they began in earnest the arduous task of spreading the Gospel in a hostile world. Inspired as they were by the Holy Spirit, they esteemed nothing more glorious than to suffer persecution or even death for the faith of Jesus Christ. Their mission has left an indelible impress on history, and today other missionaries, their successors, in distant climes continue to carry on the divine work of bringing the message of the Gospel to the nations "that sit in darkness and in the shadow of death."

Occupying the apse on the Gospel, or north, side of the Church is the Altar of the Holy Ghost, Third Person of the Most Holy Trinity. Below the tabernacle of this Altar, constructed of Botticino marble and mosaics, one reads the carved inscription: *"O quam bonus et suavis est Domine Spiritus Tuus"*—"O how good and sweet, Lord, is Thy Spirit!"

Around the Altar and filling the elevated apse in which it stands, is a bas-relief panel, harmonizing with the other Altars in the Church. Directly above the Altar is the figure of a Dove, symbolizing the Holy Ghost, surrounded by rays of celestial glory, while

Left: NORTH APSE AND ALTAR OF THE HOLY GHOST

angels offer adoring homage. On the Gospel side is represented the scene in the life of Christ by the Lake of Tiberias, when He sent His disciples forth to preach the Gospel.

The opposite portion of the panel depicts St. Francis of Assisi, faithful imitator of Jesus Christ, blessing his followers as they set out to carry the Gospel tidings into strange lands.

It is appropriate that our Church have an Altar especially dedicated to the Holy Ghost, since the Franciscan Order is primarily a missionary institution, whose missionaries, like so many Apostles, go to distant shores to preach the love of God to the nations which know Him not.

The Lady Chapel

"Fear not, Mary, for thou hast found grace with God." (St. Luke i, 30.)

DEVOTION to the Mother of Christ is as old as Christianity itself. We find her picture held in veneration in the Catacombs of the primitive Church, and it was an Angel of God who declared her to be "full of grace."

There is scarcely a Catholic Church in the world which has not an Altar dedicated to God in commemoration of the Virgin Mary, or in which she is not represented by at least a statue or a picture. The architectural designation for the Chapel of the Blessed Virgin has long been "The Lady Chapel," which quaint and lovely name heads this chapter. One may discern in the adoption of Lady Chapels, crucifixes, altars, and other ancient usages, by Protestant churches, a yearning for these customs of Catholic antiquity.

Under the eminent title of the Immaculate Conception, the Madonna is represented in our Chapel by the beautiful statue which adorns the Altar. Panels at the sides depict Mary's Presentation in the Temple, and her Coronation in Heaven.

It is appropriate here to explain briefly the teaching of the Catholic Church regarding veneration of the Blessed Virgin Mary, and of the other Saints. The Church has never permitted—much less taught—her children to adore the Saints, who are creatures like ourselves. But she bids us reverence and venerate them, because by the goodness of their lives they have endeared themselves to God, Whom they served on

The Altar of the Blessed Mother

earth, many as Martyrs with their very life-blood. We invoke the Saints, asking them who are in the glory of the Beatific Presence of God to pray for us and to implore in our behalf the things which we need in this mortal life, in fulfillment of the words of the Creed: "I believe in the communion of Saints."

The title "Mother of God," frequently misunderstood by those ignorant of its actual meaning—like the Immaculate Conception, which refers to Mary's freedom from original sin and not to the Virgin-Birth of Christ—is very ancient. Already long in use, it was formally promulgated by the Third Ecumenical Council, held at Ephesus in 431. In the sense that Christ, Second Person of the Blessed Trinity, possesses a Divine and a Human Nature, Mary, as the Mother of His Humanity, is truly the "Mother of God."

Catholics reverence the Saints because they loved God; Catholics love her whom the Eternal Father chose to be the Virgin Mother of Christ because Jesus loved her.

THE ALTAR OF SAINT ANTHONY

Chapel of St. Anthony

"Beloved of God and men, whose memory is in benediction." (Ecclesiasticus xlv, 1.)

OPPOSITE the Lady Chapel is the one dedicated to God in memory of St. Anthony of Padua. The beautiful statue represents the Saint holding in his arms the Infant Jesus, and at the sides two relief panels show him healing the sick and giving bread to the poor.

St. Anthony, who was born in Lisbon, Portugal, in 1195, died in 1231 at Padua, near Venice. He has been rightly called "the eldest son of St. Francis," for he inherited the spirit of his Seraphic Father in its sublime fullness.

After a hidden life, he suddenly came into prominence by his inspired eloquence, his wonderful knowledge of Holy Scripture, his truly Seraphic spirit, his kindness, and the power of working miracles. Nature had no bounds for the works which he wrought for the glory of God. The great devotion to him throughout the Church, and even outside its fold, is ample testimony of his heaven-given powers in our own day and age.

The Altar of the Sacred Heart

The Sacred Heart Altar

"Learn of Me, because I am meek and humble of heart." (St. Matthew xi, 29.)

DEVOTION to the Heart of Jesus, transfixed with a lance on the Cross for love of man, is as ancient as the Church which He founded. Veneration of Our Divine Lord in this most lovable of His human attributes—compassion—characterized the Franciscan Order from its earliest days. St. Bonaventure, who died in 1274, says, in a loving tribute to the Heart of the Saviour, which the Church has incorporated into her Office of Matins:

"In this Temple, this Holy of Holies, this Ark of the Testament, I will adore and praise the Name of the Lord, saying with David: I have found my heart that I might pray to my God. Yes, I have found the Heart of my King and my Lord, of my Brother and my Friend, of my most benign Jesus! Draw me, Jesus, entirely to Thy Sacred Heart. Although the wickedness of my sins should prevent it, yet Thy Heart in Its unlimited charity is open to receive me. Thou most beautiful of all hearts, Who alone canst make clean the unclean, wash me yet more from my iniquity, and purify me from my sins that I may approach Thee, Who art most pure, and grant that I may dwell in Thy Heart all the days of my life."

In the apse opposite that of the Holy Ghost stands the elevated Altar dedicated to the Sacred Heart of Jesus, symbolizing His love for humanity. The Altar bears the inscription: "*Cor Jesu, Caritatis Victimam,*

Venite Adoremus!"—"Come, let us adore the Heart of Jesus, Victim of love!"

The relief panel here represents Our Divine Lord as the "King and Center of All Hearts" enthroned above the Altar, while before Him kneel St. Francis and St. Clare—two great imitators of Him Who said, "Learn of Me because I am meek and humble of heart." (*St. Matthew xi, 29.*) The left side of the panel shows the Upper Room where, the doors being shut, the Risen Lord appeared to His disciples, and calling Thomas, bade him touch His Wounds, "being not incredulous but believing."

Opposite is depicted a contemporary nobleman venerating the Stigmata of the Five Wounds on the body of St. Francis, while surrounding the bier are the bereaved Brethren of the Holy Founder. Above his lifeless form is seen that Cross from which Christ, long years before, bade the youthful Francis go and repair His House. Certainly he had obeyed, and truly was his work well done.

The Statues

"In holiness and justice before Him all our days."
(St. Luke i, 75.)

IN THE course of this visit to the Shrines of the Church, a number of statues are seen, in addition to those on the Altars. They recall, for the most part, men and women of various epochs and walks of life who bear to the Kingdom of God much the same relation that civic heroes do to the people of a nation. It is for the same reason that the Church erects monuments to their memory—to remind posterity of their virtues, and to propose them as models.

Near the front entrance of the Church, beneath the Sanctuary of Calvary, are two wood-carved groups, representing in a touching manner the Scourging of Our Lord, and the Crowning with Thorns.

Other statues in the Church are:

The Sacred Heart of Jesus, in which the Redeemer is depicted as revealing His Heart, symbol of His love for us;

St. Patrick, Bishop and Apostle of Ireland, who lived in the 5th century and evangelized the country of which he is the Patron;

St. Benedict "the Moor," a Franciscan Brother of the 16th century, who was at one time a slave, indicated by the broken chain which he holds;

St. Teresa of Avila, a Carmelite nun, who lived in the 16th century and was renowned for her pious and learned writings;

St. Rita of Cascia, an Augustinian nun who died in the 15th century, and who is called "Saint of the Impossible," because of the great favors obtained through her intercession;

St. Teresa of the Child Jesus, widely and affectionately known as the "Little Flower," who died in France in 1897, and was canonized in 1925. This young Carmelite Sister has brought sainthood nearer to our own day, and made it more real to a busy modern world;

St. Francis of Assisi, from the well-known statue by Della Robbia, and whose life is related elsewhere in these pages;

St. Clare of Assisi, who lived at the time of St. Francis in the 13th century, and was the Foundress of the Poor Clares, an austere body of Franciscan Sisters.

St. Louis IX, King of France, Holy Land Crusader, and Patron of the Third Order of St. Francis, bearing the Crown of Thorns.

The Votive Lamps

"That a lamp may burn always in the Tabernacle."
(Exodus xxvii, 20-21.)

LIKE angelic sentinels before the Throne of the Most High, Votive Lamps are ever burning in this House of God. Their varied colors, in themselves without significance, blend with the hallowed light of the sacred edifice, and in the deep silence of night cast somber shadows among arches and pillars and Shrines, as they keep their silent vigil for a sleeping world.

Lights have been employed in the Divine worship from earliest times. As in the Old Testament the sacred seven-branched candlestick illumined the Holy of Holies of the Temple in Jerusalem, so in the New Testament from the days of the Catacombs, the Catholic Church has made use of lights in her Sacred Liturgy. Alike in great Cathedral and lowly mission Chapel, a lamp burns always before the Altar whereon reposes the Saviour of the World, concealed by His own miracle beneath the Eucharistic species, even as He concealed His Divinity beneath frail humanity in Bethlehem nineteen centuries ago. After the Church emerged from the Catacombs, and lights at the Liturgy were no longer of necessity or utility, they were used as a sign of joy and solemnity. St. Jerome, who lived in Bethlehem in the fourth century, writes that in all the Churches lights were used when the Gospel was read, even after sunrise, not to dispel the darkness, but as a visible sign of joy.

The lights burning here before these Shrines dedicated to God's heroes—the Saints—may be likened to flowers placed at the shrines of a nation's heroes. Of this outward evidence of interior devotion, a Dominican has beautifully written: "Those little flames are incessantly speaking to Christ for those who lighted them on the Altar. No one knows who lighted those little red lamps. It is a secret between the Master and loving souls, and only the Master understands what they tell Him. And the voices of those lamps—like the harmony which comes out of the melodious pipes of an immense organ in an old Gothic cathedral—some of them are pleading, some are thanking, some are weeping lowly and sighing, some are crying for mercy, for help, for protection, for grace. Those lamps are the voices of unfortunate hearts, of repentent souls, of troubled consciences hungry and thirsty for a ray of happiness, for pardon, for peace. They stand there for tired lives whose unknown history is one of suffering and torture, whose path is the path of a long, steep Calvary covered with thorns that make them bleed and agonize."

The Grotto of Nazareth

"And He went down with them, and came to Nazareth, and was subject to them." (St. Luke ii, 51.)

NAZARETH, which, according to St. Jerome, means "a flower," is a little town in Galilee, some sixty miles north of Jerusalem. It is not mentioned in the Old Testament, and seemingly had no great reputation, for Nathanael asked, "Can any thing of good come from Nazareth?" (St. John i, 46.)

A poetic charm surrounds the name of Nazareth. The message of the Angel, the Incarnation, the boyhood and youth of Jesus, the life of the Holy Family, all these subjects are vividly recalled by the little Galilean town. From there the *Ave Maria* resounded over the entire world, and now daily echoes from the lips of millions of devout Catholics who call Mary "blessed."

With these sentiments should one approach the Grotto that brings to mind the place where the "Word was made flesh," and where Jesus "advanced in wisdom and age before God and man."

According to tradition, the house in which the Holy Family lived was built against a natural cave, which thus formed an inner household apartment. This arrangement is found to this day in some of the poorer homes of Nazareth. Tradition relates that the Blessed Virgin was engaged in prayer in the Grotto when the Angel appeared to her and greeted her with the words: "Hail, full of grace, the Lord is with thee, blessed art thou among women." (*St. Luke* i, 28.)

At the foot of the large stairway is the Chapel of

the Angel, where there are two Altars. The one at the right hand is dedicated to St. Joseph, the painting depicting the Saint instructing the youthful Christ. The one at the left commemorates St. Anne, who is represented teaching her child Mary. Two steps lead into the Grotto where stands the Altar of the Annunciation, which in Nazareth marks the place where the Archangel Gabriel announced to Mary that she would be the Mother of the Saviour. Underneath the Altar is a stone from Nazareth. The Altar piece, representing the mystery of this holy place, is a copy of Luca Della Robbia's famous work, "The Annunciation."

At the left of this Altar is reproduced a curious feature of the original Chapel, a fragment of a granite column hanging from the roof. In 1638, African Moors in search of possible hidden treasure cut the column in two, leaving the upper portion suspending from the masonry of the ceiling. A part of another smaller shaft has been placed beneath this.

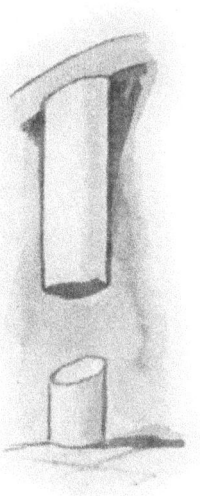

At the Epistle or right side of the Altar of the Annunciation, a doorway opens into the rear part of the Grotto, which contains an Altar dedicated to St. Joseph, above which is a painting of the Saint with the Child Jesus.

So careful has the reproduction of this Holy Shrine been made, that even the stone-work is copied with which the natural rock ceiling of the Grotto was once repaired.

Left: THE GROTTO OF
THE ANNUNCIATION

A Vista in the Catacombs

The Catacombs

"Blessed are they that suffer persecution for justice sake." (St. Matthew v, 10.)

WHILE the bloodthirsty Nero was gloating over the destruction of Rome and washing his hands in the blood of Christians, an unknown Commonwealth was forming itself around the seat of paganism, destined to overthrow its idols and to emerge from the earth to occupy the Throne of the Caesars.

This subterranean "Republic" was formed in the Catacombs, where the early Christians buried their martyrs, and assembled in the dark of night for the celebration of the divine worship.

We can form an idea of the extent of this immense necropolis which, like a network, encircled the city of Rome, when we consider that the length of the Catacombs has been variously estimated at 600 to 900 miles, of which perhaps not one-third has been explored up to the present. The bodies interred in the Catacombs (in Latin *cœmeterium*, from the Greek κοιμητήριον—a place of rest) number some six millions.

These subterranean galleries were in places three, four, and even five, stories deep, and generally from four to five feet wide.

The bodies were laid to rest in niches in the walls and the openings closed with slabs of marble or stone, upon which an epitaph was inscribed. In some places cubicula, or large chapels, were set apart for families or martyrs of distinction.

A study of the Catacombs, their inscriptions, and pictorial representations, gives convincing proof that the doctrines of the Catholic Church today are the same as those of the Church in the Catacombs, when her children suffered and laid down their lives in testimony of their devotion to those same principles of faith in which the Catholics of this century firmly believe. The Catacombs are indeed irrefutable proof of the divine institution and truth of our Holy Mother Church, for there we find represented the Holy Eucharist and the other Sacraments, the Sign of the Cross, the veneration of the Mother of Christ and of the Saints, and the supremacy of St. Peter and his successors. The six millions of Christians buried there lived and died for this faith and testify to "Jesus Christ, yesterday, and today, and the same forever." (*Hebrews xiii, 8.*)

In the beautiful story "Fabiola," by Cardinal Wiseman, we are given a realistic and striking picture of the life and faith of the early Christians, together with a vivid description of the Catacombs.

Our catacombs are faithful copies of those in Rome; and these bare walls seem to say, as we read some of the epitaphs: "*Sta, Viator*—Stand a little while, O Wanderer"—pause and consider the price at which thou hast been redeemed!

The Martyr's Crypt

"I saw under the altar the souls of them that were slain for the Word of God." (Apocalypse vi, 9.)

THIS subterranean catacomb Chapel, circular in form, is like many found in those maze-like hiding-places of the early Christians. The relics of St. Benignus, brought from the Roman Catacombs, are encased in the wax figure beneath the Altar. The earthly remains of this early Christian Martyr were transferred from the Cathedral at Narni, in Italy, to Mount Saint Sepulchre at the time of its foundation, and are reminders to us of the many persecutions and hardships amid which the first Christians professed their faith.

The decorations are in the ancient style of the Catacombs. In the niche the Saviour is represented with His hand raised in blessing. Before the Altar are paintings representing St. Stephen, the first Martyr, and St. Benignus, who is here buried.

The early Catacomb pictures held deep religious meanings, and these symbols, copied from the originals in the Catacombs of Rome, are examples of the more important ones. The inscriptions are usually in Greek, the liturgical language in Rome until after the second century. Beginning at the lower left corner above the Altar, they are:

The Phoenix, symbol of the resurrection of the body;

Alpha and Omega Monogram, A ⲱ (or A Ω) meaning "The First and the Last—the Beginning and the End";

The Anchor, with the inscription IHCOTC XPICTOC, or IHΣOΥΣ XPIΣTOΣ (Jesus Christ), symbol of Christ, our hope. (The frequently seen monogram "I H S" is composed of the first three letters of the word Jesus in Greek: IHΣOΥΣ);

The Church, symbolized as a tree, bearing fruit and sheltering a lamb;

The White Dove, symbol of innocence;

The center monogram, consisting of the interwoven Greek letters X and P (*chi* and *rho*), used in the Catacombs from the beginning of the second century, are the first two letters of the word XPIΣTOΣ, or Christ;

The Dove of Peace, bearing an olive-branch;

The Banner of Christ conquering the evil one, represented by a serpent, with the inscription EN TOΥTΩ NIKA, "In This Conquer";

A tablet inscribed ZHCEC, or ZHΣEΣ, "Thou Shalt Live," a symbol of steadfast faith;

The Fish, a symbol of Christ in ancient times, the Greek word IXΘΥΣ (Fish) being composed of the initial letters of the words Jesus Christ, Son

of God, Saviour ('Ιησοῦς Χριστός Θεοῦ Υἱός Σωτήρ);
The Triangle, symbolizing the Holy Trinity;
The Lamb, symbol of Christ, standing on the rock from which flow four fountains, figuring the Four Gospels, whence come the waters of salvation.

From this crypt a short passageway leads to the Chapel of Purgatory.

The Purgatory Chapel

"Restrain not grace from the dead."
(Ecclesiasticus vii, 37.)

THIS Chapel dedicated to the memory of the Faithful Departed is in a special manner intended to remind us of the fleeting character of this life, and of death which must inevitably end our days. The funereal decorations and the paintings, where the thought of death alternates with that of the resurrection, remind us of the words of Solomon: "Vanity of vanities and all is vanity!" (*Ecclesiastes* i, 2.)

Death is a terror to all, and spares no class of society, no age, no calling in life, no spiritual nor temporal authority. Suddenly and without warning it comes to men without regard to circumstances; the individual that is summoned must obey the fatal call and begin his march to the grave. But death, so formidable to those who have set their hearts on the treasures and pleasures of this life, becomes a warm friend and a welcome liberator to him who considers this visitor in his real quality as a messenger of God. Death leads on to resurrection. From this vale of tears it transports unto the realms of eternal bliss.

At the black marble Altar in this Chapel, the Holy Sacrifice of the Mass is offered to God in behalf of the Faithful "who have gone before us with the Sign of Faith and who sleep the sleep of peace," as beautifully expressed in the words of the ancient Canon of the Mass.

The painting on the left wall represents the lifeless body of Christ, "the first begotten of the dead,"

Left: THE CHAPEL OF
THE FAITHFUL DEPARTED

(*Apocalypse* i, 5) taken down from the Cross, as His Mother looks with grief upon her Divine Son, mutilated by the cruelty of those whom He had befriended.

Opposite is represented the vision of the Prophet Ezechiel, to whom the Lord showed a plain filled with bones, saying: "Prophesy concerning these dry bones, and say to them: 'Ye dry bones, hear ye the word of the Lord.' " And the prophet prophesied, and behold, a commotion, and the bones came together, each one to its joint. And he prophesied again, and the spirit came into them and they lived: and they stood upon their feet an exceeding great army. (*Ezechiel xxxvii*.)

Behind the Altar, at the left, is represented the spectre of Death, while on the other side the Angel of God reveals Eternal Life, symbolized by the Cross above the heavenly Jerusalem, conveying the thought that through Death we enter into Everlasting Life. The two paintings near the entrance to the Chapel show Christ raising Lazarus, and Tobias burying the dead.

All these representations bring before the mind the certainty of death and the memory of those who, although actually free from guilt of sin, are detained in the ante-room of heaven until they have atoned "so as by fire" (I *Corinthians* iii, 15) for the lesser faults and shortcomings that keep them from the company of the Blessed before the Throne of God.

To the Catholic heart bowed down in grief, it is a consoling thought that the great chasm between this life and eternity is spanned by prayer for dear ones separated from us by death. It is the communion of Saints: that blessed union of the Church Militant on earth to the Church Suffering, even as the invocation of the Saints in Heaven unites us to the Church Triumphant. "It is a holy and wholesome thought to

pray for the dead, that they may be loosed from sins."
(II *Machabees xii*, 46.)

As the astronomer gazes through his telescope into the starry world above and discovers wonders invisible to the naked eye, so the Saints, bent on unraveling the mysteries of eternity, discover through the dark valley of death those beautiful shores of which the Apostle says: "Eye hath not seen, nor ear heard, neither hath it entered into the heart of man, what things God hath prepared for them that love Him." (*I Corinthians ii*, 9.)

Catacomb Chapel of Saint Sebastian, Soldier-Martyr

The Catacomb Chapels

"Whosoever killeth you, will think that he doth a service to God." (St. John xvi, 2.)

PASSING through the doorway behind the Purgatory Chapel Altar, one enters a continuation of the Catacombs. The mural paintings in the two stairways of the first room represent the early Martyrs, St. Venatius and St. Thecla, cast among the beasts of the arena. Continuing through a narrow passageway, the visitor comes to two Chapels typical of the larger ones, decorated with careful fidelity to the style of the Catacombs.

The Chapel to the left on entering is dedicated to St. Cecilia, Virgin and Martyr, venerated as the Patroness of Musicians. The statue beneath the Altar in the arcosolium is a copy of the one by Maderno which adorns the Saint's tomb in Rome, representing her body as it was found incorrupt centuries after her martyrdom.

The Chapel opposite is dedicated to St. Sebastian, the Soldier-Martyr. The figure here is a copy of Bernini's statue in the Church of St. Sebastian on the Appian Way near Rome, where the Saint sealed his faith with his blood.

Retracing the way through the Purgatory Chapel and the Martyr's Crypt, one follows the Catacomb passage to the right, which leads to the Nativity Grotto.

Catacomb Chapel of Saint Cecilia, Virgin and Martyr

The Grotto of Bethlehem

"Let us go over to Bethlehem and see this word that is come to pass." (St. Luke ii, 15.)

BETHLEHEM, formerly called Ephrata, is often mentioned in Holy Scripture, and the lives of Jacob, Ruth, and David are intimately connected with the little town, out of which came forth the Ruler of Israel. The dawn of the Redemption broke from there over the world when, at the time of Caesar Augustus, the days were accomplished and Christ the Lord was born in the City of David. And ever since, the eyes of Christendom have rested on that peaceful little town. St. Helena, Imperial Mother of Constantine, erected a beautiful Basilica over the lowly stable, which, according to the custom of the country, and the testimony of St. Justin the Martyr of the second century, was a grotto where the shepherds sheltered their flocks in the cold and rainy days of winter. This venerable Basilica of the fourth century stands there today, the oldest Christian church in the world.

The Sacred Grotto is faithfully represented here as it exists now in Bethlehem. In the semicircular niche between the two stairways is the representation of the birthplace of the Saviour, indicated by a silvered star beneath the Altar, bearing the inscription: *"Hic de Virgine Maria Jesus Christus natus est"*—"Here Jesus Christ was born of the Virgin Mary." A marble slab forms the altar table, and in the niche is a figure of the Infant Jesus surrounded by a glory of angels.

At the right there is a little recess in the Grotto, where the shepherds of old were wont to put the feed

for their animals. In this humble manger the Blessed Virgin placed the Infant Saviour of the world, as related in the Gospel of St. Luke.

Here it was that the shepherds came to pay their homage to the Divine Child. Here too occurred the adoration by the Wise Men of the East, commemorated now by a marble Altar known as the Altar of the Wise Men, above which is a painting of "The Adoration of the Magi."

On Christmas Eve the same impressive midnight ceremonies, which in Bethlehem commemorate the Nativity of Christ, take place in this Grotto. After the Midnight Mass, a Figure of the Infant Jesus is carried here in solemn procession, and reverently placed on the silvered star, like the one sacred to Our Lord's Birth. The Gospel of Christmas is chanted by the Deacon, who pauses to transfer the Figure to the Manger at the words: "She brought forth her first-born Son, and wrapped Him up in swaddling clothes, and laid Him in a manger, because there was no room for them in the inn." (*St. Luke* ii, 7.)

As in Bethlehem, two winding stairways lead from the Crypt to the Church above. Ascending, one is again surrounded by the beauty of the upper Church, where a lingering gaze takes farewell of the Shrines of this peaceful House of God.

Retracing his way through the Sacristy, the pilgrim pauses to write his name in the Visitors' Register there, in the volumes of which other pilgrims, of many creeds and titles and nationalities, have inscribed their names in the years gone by.

Leaving the Monastery portal, the visitor walks a short distance and, passing through the arched Rosary Portico, comes to the outdoor Shrines.

Left: THE BETHLEHEM GROTTO

The Manger

The Valley and Grotto of Gethsemane

"Then Jesus came with them into . . . Gethsemane." (St. Matthew xxvi, 36.)

AS THE Pilgrim stands on the brow of the steep hill overlooking Gethsemane Valley, there is unfolded to his sight a charming vista. As if in a setting of precious stones, among trees and flowers and lawns are seen other Shrines, which help to keep in mind the Eternal Truths so eloquently proclaimed by the Holy Places in the Church just visited.

About midway down the hillside walk is the Grotto of Gethsemane, a replica of the one near the Garden of Olives in Jerusalem, dedicated to Our Lord's Agony on the eve of His Crucifixion. This natural Grotto in the Valley of Josaphat, little changed in appearance since the time of Christ, has long been a venerated Shrine.

Here in the evening, with His disciples, the Saviour was wont to come, weary from His labors for souls. In this quiet spot at the foot of Olivet, He would pass the night in prayer to His Heavenly Father. "And going out, He went, according to His custom, to the Mount of Olives." (*St. Luke xxii*, 39.) On the night of His betrayal He left some of His Apostles in this Grotto, and taking Peter, James, and John, He went out among the olive trees and prostrated Himself in prayer. There, as God, He saw the untold millions of sins, from that of Adam down to the end of time, and the sufferings and ingratitude which He was to endure. Then, in the anguish of His Sacred Heart, His sweat became as

drops of blood, and He cried out: "My Father, if it be possible, let this chalice pass from me. Nevertheless, not as I will, but as Thou wilt!" (*St. Matthew xxvi*, 39.)

There the shameful betrayal of his Master by Judas' treacherous kiss took place. "And he that betrayed Him, gave them a sign, saying: Whomsoever I shall kiss, that is He, hold Him fast. And forthwith coming to Jesus, he said: 'Hail, Rabbi.' And he kissed Him." (*St. Matthew xxvi*, 48-49.)

The panel above the Altar here portrays the Divine Saviour comforted in His Agony by an Angel.

Over the place sanctified by Our Saviour's Agony in the Garden of Gethsemane, with the help chiefly of the Catholics of the United States, the Franciscans have built a beautiful Church, following the architectural lines of the primitive Basilica erected there in the fourth century.

Left: IN THE VALLEY OF GETHSEMANE

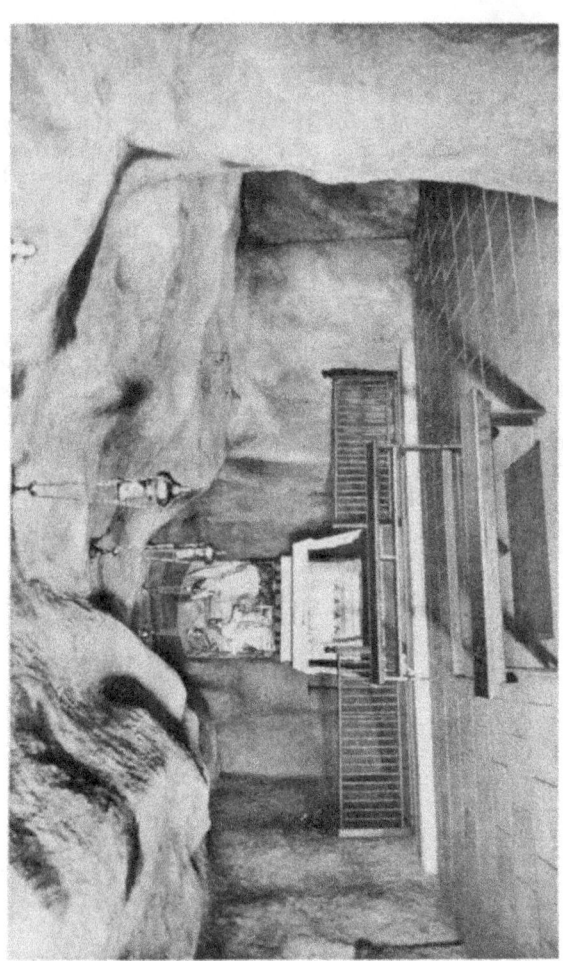

The Gethsemane Grotto

The Tomb of the Blessed Virgin

"And a great sign appeared in heaven: A woman clothed with the sun, and the moon under her feet, and on her head a crown of twelve stars."
(Apocalypse xii, 1.)

ON COMING from the Grotto of Gethsemane, one passes to the near-by Tomb of the Blessed Virgin, as in the Holy Land. In Jerusalem this Shrine is held in great veneration, not only by Christians, but even by Mohammedans, who acknowledge that the Mother of Jesus deserves the reverence and love of mankind.

In the large room which contains the Tomb, built in the form of a mausoleum, a mural painting above the Altar represents the Blessed Virgin, surrounded by Angels, kneeling before her Divine Son, Who crowns her as Queen of Heaven.

At the right, entered through a low door, is the Tomb. Inside is represented a burial slab covered with marble, above which are hanging lamps and a Byzantine painting of Our Blessed Lady and her Divine Child. This Shrine is a replica of that holy place where the sinless body of the Virgin Mother of Christ was reverently laid by the Apostles when she had departed this life.

According to a very ancient tradition, recognized by the Fourth Ecumenical Council held in Chalcedon in 451, after the burial of the Blessed Virgin, the Apostles heard heavenly melodies around her Tomb, as if sung

THE TOMB OF THE BLESSED VIRGIN

by Angel voices. Shortly thereafter, on opening the sepulchre at the earnest request of one of their number who was not present at the burial, the grave was found empty. From this the Apostles understood that the immaculate body of the Virgin Mother of their Divine Master had been miraculously preserved from corruption and assumed into Heaven.

On the Feast of the Assumption of the Blessed Virgin, August 15, 1917, Solemn High Mass was celebrated for the first time at this Shrine, dedicating it to God's honor.

THE GROTTO OF LOURDES

The Grotto of Lourdes

"Thou art all fair . . . and there is not a spot in thee." (Canticle iv, 7.)

THE little Pyrenean town of Lourdes in the south of France is famed throughout the world. Millions of Pilgrims have gathered there from all parts of the globe to pray at the Grotto in which the Blessed Virgin, as the Immaculate Conception, appeared to a fourteen-year-old peasant girl named Bernadette Soubiroux, now St. Bernadette. The first of eighteen apparitions occurred on the 11th of February, 1858. This mysterious vision was that of a young and fair Lady, described as "lovelier than I have ever seen," by the favored Bernadette. It was only after four years, when the apparitions had been fully established by a continuous series of miracles, that their authenticity was admitted by the Church.

Since then no other Shrine has attracted such throngs. According to statistics published in a secular paper, over 35,000,000 pilgrims and visitors of all denominations came to the Shrine of Lourdes between 1858 and 1933, while the average number of visitors annually at present is one million. Over four thousand wonderful cures occurred at the Shrine in the first fifty years of the pilgrimages. The certificates of these maladies and cures can be inspected by all physicians at the *Bureau des Contestations*, of which a sceptical review, the *Annales des Sciences Physiques*, in the course of an article on this subject, says: "On reading it, unprejudiced minds cannot but be convinced that the facts stated are authentic." No natural cause, known or unknown, is sufficient to account for the marvelous cures witnessed at the celebrated rock where the Virgin Mother of Christ deigned to appear. They can only be from the intervention of God.

The miraculous happenings at Lourdes have prompted the faithful of every land to transplant into their own climes replicas of the Holy Grotto of the Pyrenees. In this Gethsemane Valley is held in veneration this faithful replica of the famed Lourdes Grotto, once unknown in the obscurity of a little French village. A myriad of white and red roses enhances the beauty of this charming spot, where nature, ever dear to the Sons of St. Francis, vies with man in embellishing these Shrines sacred to the memory of Our Lord and His Saints. High above the Grotto Altar is a niche which enshrines the figure of Our Lady of the Immaculate Conception.

This Grotto was solemnly dedicated, amid a great concourse of people, on the 15th of August, 1913, the Feast of the Assumption of the Blessed Virgin, by the late Most Rev. Charles W. Currier, Bishop of Matanzas, Cuba.

CHAPEL OF THE HOLY FAMILY

House of the Holy Family and Chapel of St. Anne

"Arise, and take the Child and His mother, and fly into Egypt." (St. Matthew ii, 13.)

AT THE far end of the Gethsemane Valley is a reproduction of the Shrine which marks the traditional place where the Holy Family remained in Egypt during the persecution of Herod. The belief that the Child Jesus, with Mary and Joseph, lived in Babylon, now Old Cairo, is founded on the apocryphal "Gospel of the Infancy of Our Lord," and supported by an uninterrupted tradition. In earliest times, the

THE CHAPEL OF ST. ANNE

Christians built there a Church in honor of that event. The Franciscans came into possession of the Church in the seventeenth century, but, owing to fanatical persecution, they were forced to abandon it. Today the Church and Crypt are in the hands of the schismatic Copts.

This Crypt is modelled after the original and gives a good example of Coptic architecture, evident in the curious small Altar and the Coptic crosses of the pillar capitals.

Above the CRYPT IS THE CHAPEL OF ST. ANNE, mother of the Blessed Virgin. Here a statue of this holy exemplar of maternal love, holding her blessed child, stands above an Altar which is surmounted by a dome. Situated at the extremity of the beautiful Valley, this little Oratory adds much to the grace and beauty of this heavenly spot.

The Way of the Cross

"And bearing His own cross, He went forth to that place which is called Calvary." (St. John xix, 17.)

AMID the natural beauties of this Valley are seen the outdoor Stations of the Way of the Cross—eloquent monuments to the sufferings of the Redeemer. As one looks upon these representations of Our Lord's all-atoning Sacrifice, the words of the Prophet Jeremias come to mind: "All ye that pass by the way, attend and see if there be any sorrow like to my sorrow." (*Lamentations* i, 12.)

In Jerusalem, the Way of the Cross is followed along the *Via Dolorosa*, or Way of Sorrow, every Friday. Led by the Franciscan Guardians of the Holy Places, pilgrims and visitors assist at this unique devotion, so consoling to him who realizes that he is praying in the very places sanctified by the scenes of the First Good Friday, commemorated by continuous venerable traditions.

The Way of the Cross is truly and appropriately of Franciscan origin. This beautiful devotion to the sacred memorials of Christ's Passion and Death was introduced into Europe by the Franciscans, who in 1219 were established in Palestine by their Founder, St. Francis of Assisi. Returning from Palestine, members of the Order built replicas of those scenes in their Churches and Chapels. The Holy See approved this devotion, and in 1686 Pope Innocent XI granted to these memorials the same Indulgences as were to be gained by visiting the Holy Places in Jerusalem. To the Sons of St. Francis we owe the fact that today the

Left: JERUSALEM
FROM MT. OLIVET

Way of the Cross is traced for us in grove and cloister, in church and chapel and cemetery, throughout the world.

The artistic panels here, representing scenes of Our Lord's Passion and Death, were given by those generous donors whose names are inscribed on the respective Stations. They were blessed on Good Friday, 1916, when the Way of the Cross took place in this Valley. This yearly custom has continued, and is attended by ever-increasing numbers, who are thus eloquently reminded of the price paid for man's Redemption by Our Divine Saviour amid cruelest sufferings. Day by day, throughout the year, it is edifying to observe visitors pausing in silent prayer as they pass from Station to Station, wending their way up the hillside.

SHORT MEDITATIONS FOR THE STATIONS OF THE CROSS

I

"Away with Him!" the impious rabble cry;
Yet, Jesus, 'twas my sins that bade Thee die.

II

Bent 'neath the heavy Cross, Our Lord begins
His last sad journey, heavier pressed my sins.

III

Cruel! They torture Him and scoff the more,
When, faint and pale, He falls. My soul adore.

IV

Dreading the sight on which her soul is set,
She waits, and—bitter joy!—their eyes have met.

V

Eager would I the precious burden share,
Which Simon, loathing, soon is glad to bear.

VI

Full of fond pity, full of faith e'en now,
Veronica wipes tenderly the bleeding brow.

VII
'Gainst the steep hill He totters on with pain,
O God!—that yell—He falls, He falls again!

VIII
Hush, mourning daughters of Jerusalem!
Weep not for Me; your children, weep for them.

IX
Is it that night of woe in Caiphas' halls,
The scourging, thorns, or Cross—that thrice He falls.

X
Jeers and foul jests doth He, the All-Holy, bear,
While fiends from virgin limbs the garments tear.

XI
Lewd ruffians fling Him on His bed of death;
The nails pierce deep. "Father forgive!" He saitl

XII
More love there is not, nor more agony;
So Jesus dies. For me—He dies for me!

XIII
Nigh to the Cross she stood till all was done
And now the Mother's arms have clasped her Son.

XIV
Oh! hard Thy rock-hewn grave, more hard my heart!
Yet here Thou lov'st to dwell. Come, Lord, and never part.

Chapel of the Ascension

"Whilst He blessed them, He departed from them and was carried up to Heaven." (St. Luke xxiv, 51.)

THE Chapel of the Ascension commemorates Our Lord's last farewell, as He took His earthly departure from His Apostles. Built on the height above the Grotto of Lourdes, it crowns the hilltop, as the original Chapel commands the summit of Mount Olivet, overlooking the Holy City of Jerusalem.

This Chapel is a replica of the one built by the Crusaders in the thirteenth century over the site of the original fourth century Ascension Shrine. In the center of the Chapel there is a square marble Altar, beneath which is reproduced the rock upon which tradition says Our Lord stood on that First Ascension Thursday.

This graceful arched Chapel is constructed of crushed marbles and stones of delicate hues, in harmony with the near-by Rosary Portico. The interior of the lofty dome is decorated with a Byzantine allegorical representation of the Ascension, composed of figures of Christ and the Apostles.

The solemn blessing of this Chapel took place on the Feast of the Ascension, 1925, and Holy Mass is celebrated here on Ascension Thursday, and other occasions.

Left: THE CHAPEL OF THE ASCENSION AND ONE OF THE STATIONS OF THE CROSS

The Portiuncula Chapel

"I have chosen and have sanctified this place, that my name may be there forever."
(II Paralipomenon vii, 16.)

BEFORE leaving the Monastery grounds, the pilgrim may visit the Chapel of Portiuncula, also called St. Mary of the Angels, situated to the north of the Church, within the enclosure of the Portico. It is a reproduction in rough Potomac stone of the famous Chapel of that name near Assisi, in Italy.

The origin of that Shrine is lost in the dim obscurity of the centuries. An ancient tradition says that it was built by four holy men, who came from Palestine and settled in the plains of Umbria about the year 352. They called it the Chapel of St. Mary, because of their veneration for her Tomb in Jerusalem, of which they brought with them a fragment which they placed in the Chapel. Later, the Benedictines obtained possession of the Shrine, calling it the Chapel of St. Mary of the Portiuncula, or "Little Portion." It also acquired the name of St. Mary of the Angels, because the voices of Angels were said to have been heard there praising God. It was offered to St. Francis and his first companions by the Benedictines in 1209. St. Francis would receive it only as a loan, and insisted on sending to the Benedictine Abbot of Monte Subasio an annual rental of a basket of fish. As a mark of gracious courtesy, the Abbot would send back a quantity of olive oil for a receipt.

Besides being the *alma mater* of all Franciscan Churches, the Chapel of St. Mary of the Angels is famed especially for the great Indulgence of the

Left: THE PORTIUNCULA CHAPEL

Portiuncula granted to St. Francis by Pope Honorius III in 1216.

Our Chapel is a reproduction of the Shrine as it was in the time of St. Francis, without the decorations added in later years. The rugged construction, the heavy walls and arched ceiling, the simple Altar and the wrought iron grill work, all possess a simple beauty. Over the Altar hangs a Byzantine Crucifix, and a painting of the Annunciation after the original by Hilary of Viterbo (1393). On the side walls are depicted scenes from the life of Our Lord and of St. Francis.

The Monastery Cloister

"One thing I have asked of the Lord, this will I seek after; that I may dwell in the house of the Lord all the days of my life." (Psalm xxvi, 4.)

ALTHOUGH the Cloister is not open to the general public, a chapter concerning it will be of interest. The Cloister, as its name indicates, is the portion of a Monastery enclosed or set apart as the habitation of the Religious dwelling there. Amid these peaceful surroundings, the members of the Order fulfill their daily tasks for God and souls.

Here the order of the day is observed with the precision of a well-organized body, the activities being divided between prayer and work. It may be remarked that the Franciscan Order is not *cloistered* in the sense that its members are not allowed to leave the enclosure of the Monastery. On the contrary, the Order of St. Francis has ever been one of great activity, and the special vocation of a Franciscan may be described as doing whatever the Cause of Christ demands, and going wherever he may be sent. The Franciscan is equally at home in the Orient, in the tiny village, in the busy metropolitan center, or in the remote mission. He cares for the sick and the dying on the field of battle, or he teaches in the quiet of the classroom: the whole world is his home.

In keeping with the purpose of the Monastery are the offices and library within the Cloister. In the former are carried on the extensive administrative activities connected with "THE CRUSADER'S ALMANAC," including a world-wide correspondence relating to the Holy Land and its Missions. Among the thousands of

volumes treasured in the Monastery library may be mentioned a collection of Orientalia and Franciscana, recognized as of outstanding importance by scholars. Of interest, too, are ancient tomes of early printing, and the mediaeval manuscripts, patiently and laboriously written in the Monasteries for posterity, long before the invention of printing.

The characteristic feature of the Cloister is the large quadrangle, enclosing the center courtyard or cloister garth. This is laid out in walks and flower-beds, surrounded by an arched ambulatory of simple and pleasing design, which affords a place for outdoor exercise, even in inclement weather. Its picturesque red brick walls and arches are set off by the green of palms and exotic plants during the summer months. Even in the cold of winter, when covered with a mantle of snow on a frosty, moonlit night, this spot possesses a charm and peaceful tranquillity priceless to soul and body.

In the cloistered garden back of the Monastery, a little Shrine called the Alverna Chapel has been erected to commemorate St. Francis' love for nature. It stands in a lonely grove, surrounded by tall pines and cedars, where birds love to nestle and to trill their evening vesper-song.

A walk through wooded paths leads to a rustic Chapel of St. Paschal. This little Shrine is built of stones which formed the foundations of some of the buildings of this old estate a century or more ago, when Washington was rather a dream than the magnificent reality of today. The Chapel commemorates St. Paschal Baylon, a Franciscan Brother who lived in Spain in the sixteenth century, and who, because of his almost angelic devotion to the Blessed Sacrament, was chosen by the Church as the Heavenly Patron of all Eucharistic Congresses, societies, and devotions.

Left: THE CLOISTER

The Peaceful Cemetery

It is fitting to conclude this chapter on the Cloister with mention of the Cemetery. With the knowledge that "it is a holy and wholesome thought to pray for the dead, that they may be loosed from their sins" (*II Maccabees xii, 46*), the Monastery Cemetery is "God's Acre," to which our Brethren may go in life to pray for the eternal repose of their departed Confrères. As they have done, so it is a consoling thought for them to know that, in the after years when death shall have laid them in that same graveyard, others will come to offer a silent prayer for the peace of their immortal souls. The Cemetery, dominated by a large white Cross, lies on the slope of the hill, facing the east. In this quiet spot, dotted with cedars and flowering shrubs, our departed Brethren await the great summons of the final Resurrection Day, each peaceful grave marked with a plain marble Cross, on which their names have been inscribed, even as they are written in the Book of Life.

The Purpose of the Monastery

"If I forget thee, O Jerusalem, let my right hand be forgotten." (Psalm cxxxvi, 5.)

AN EXPLANATION of the purpose of the Monastery will be appreciated by many of the visitors to these Shrines. The chief purpose of the Institution is to interest the Catholics of America and other English-speaking countries in the work of the Holy Land, which mission it carries on as "THE COMMISSARIAT OF THE HOLY LAND."

The Custody of the Holy Land in Jerusalem is represented throughout the world by some 56 Commissariats. Prior to the establishment of this one in America, the needs of the Holy Land were but little known in this country. Few fully understood the mission of preserving the Holy Shrines of our Religion, and keeping alive the Faith in those places which were hallowed by the Life and Death of the Redeemer of mankind.

Since the foundation of the American Commissariat of the Holy Land, the Catholics of this great Republic have played an increasingly important part in the vast work connected with the maintenance of the Holy Places and the Missions of Palestine. When the countries of Europe became impoverished by the World War, it was through this Institution that this great and holy work was carried on. It seemed as though the Omniscient God, peering into the future, in His Providence raised up this Monastery for that sublime purpose. It is our privileged mission to continue the

Master's work, now and during the years to come as in the past, in His own chosen vineyard, entrusted through the centuries by His earthly Vicar to Franciscan care.

During the seven hundred years in which the Sons of St. Francis have kept faithful guard at the Holy Places of Palestine, no work has been too great for them to undertake, no persecution too severe; pains and torments and death have been endured by them, and it is due to their suffering and bravery that these Shrines are now in the possession of the Catholic Church. Today the pilgrim may kneel there in veneration, assist at the Holy Sacrifice, and receive the Sacraments, which precious privilege he owes to their labors.

That this Mission may be carried on, one of the important works of the Monastery is the education and training of young men as Franciscans, who will devote their lives to the welfare and service of the Sacred Places and the Missions of the Land of Palestine.

In the days of old, the Crusaders went forth to the rescue of the Holy Land, sacrificing home and wealth, and even life itself. The day of the sword has passed and the era of peaceful methods has come in its stead. Yet the work of this mission is no less important than it was in the days of Godfrey de Bouillon and Richard the Lion-hearted, and their brave fellows who rallied under the standard of the Cross. The Shrines must still be cared for, pilgrims harbored, the orphans and the poorest of God's poor provided for, and the vast work of the Missions of the Holy Land carried on. Particulars concerning the CRUSADE FOR THE HOLY LAND, an association approved by the Holy See for the support of the Holy Places, may be obtained upon request.

The Franciscans and the World

"God hath abolished the memory of the proud, and hath preserved the memory of them that are humble."
(Ecclesiasticus x, 21.)

FEW realize how much is owed by civilization to St. Francis and the Franciscans. Many who talk about the "dark ages" and the "ignorant monks" display scant knowledge of history. Probably they never heard, for instance, of the English Franciscan Roger Bacon who died in 1292, on the occasion of the seventh centenary of whose birth Oxford University, where once he taught, erected a monument in his honor in 1914.

In his remote day, Friar Roger Bacon foretold many of the great inventions of our own age, and he foresaw the uses of steam and electricity. He wrote of what we know today as railroads and automobiles; he affirmed that man could make machines capable of flight, and even described the mechanism of these machines, thought out by himself in accordance with the knowledge of his time. In his works, the scientist of today finds astonishing discussions of astronomy, optics, light, mechanics, chemistry, and the experimental sciences. He wrote authoritatively of mathematics, tides, perspective, psychology, metaphysics, gravity, agriculture, and medicine. Bacon was no less learned in theology, philosophy, philology, grammar, logic, and music. His treatise on the rotundity of the earth was read by Columbus, who discovered it in the "*Imago Mundi*" by Petrus Alliaco, and by it he was strongly influenced in his reasoning (*Encyclopedia Britannica*). Roger Bacon foresaw and argued the necessity of the reform of the Julian Calendar three centuries before its accomplishment by Pope Gregory XIII. He described gunpowder, which he is believed to have invented in his laboratory, and he wrote of microscopes and telescopes to indicate that he must have possessed them long before their recorded invention. To him, too, is ascribed the invention of spectacles. Apparently obscure passages in some of Bacon's writings have been found to constitute elaborate codes, employing Latin, Greek, and Hebrew, embodied in a system of almost microscopic shorthand. These stenographic signs, decoded by key sentences, shed still greater luster upon the brilliant mind of this thirteenth century Friar. Much valuable research work in Bacon's code and other writings has been done under the auspices of the University of Pennsylvania, in which laboratories some of his apparently impossible chemical formulae have been found to produce the results Bacon claimed for them.

Another Franciscan, Father Marino Mersenne, who

lived in the sixteenth century, also maintained the possibility of mechanical flight.

Historians hold that the English Franciscan Friar, who, according to Mercator's Atlas, visited the North Pole about 1380 and measured that territory with an astrolabe, was Friar John Somer, a famous mathematician and astronomer of Oxford, of whom mention is made by Chaucer.

In these days of military power and skill, few know that it was Friar Berthold Schwarz who, in his laboratory, discovered the application of gunpowder to artillery.

That the first book printed in America should have been published under Franciscan auspices is consistent with the early history of printing. Gutenberg, its in-

ventor, lies buried in the Franciscan Church in Mainz, the city of his death, having been, like practically all of the early printers, a Catholic. Among these was the famous Caxton, the earliest product of whose press near Westminster Abbey was a certificate of a Papal Indulgence, printed December 13, 1476, followed by Lives of the Saints and other religious works. His first printing experience was on the Continent in connection with the Franciscan Friar Bartholomew's encyclopedia, "*De Proprietatibus Rerum,*" elsewhere mentioned. The majority of the first printed works were Catholic Bibles, theological, doctrinal, and liturgical books, under the patronage of Popes, Cardinals, and Bishops, notable among whom was the famous Franciscan Cardinal Ximenes, who used a fortune in producing the first polyglot Bible, printed in Greek, Latin, Hebrew, and Chaldaic, in 1514.

The Friars were quick to employ printing to spread the Bible, giving wide distribution to the *Biblia Pauperum,* or "Bible of the Poor," composed of quotations from the Sacred Text, illustrated with numerous woodcuts. During the first seventy years after the discovery of printing, and *prior* to Luther's German version of the New Testament in 1522, no less than 207 Catholic editions of the Bible were printed, of which the great Gutenberg Bible treasured in the Library of Congress is a notable example. Besides 156 editions of the Bible in Latin, 6 in Hebrew, and the polyglot above mentioned, there were printed during this period alone 19 editions in German, 11 in Italian, 11 in French, 2 in Bohemian, 1 in Flemish, and 1 in Russian, followed somewhat later by an English version.

The Church welcomed as a blessing the art of printing, which was to carry on the work perpetuated by innumerable and unknown Monks, whose manuscripts had preserved through the centuries the treasures of sacred and classical literature. "The Monks were not opposed to printing, as has sometimes been contended. The books of the first thirty years after the invention of the art were produced chiefly under the patronage of the Monasteries and for the use of the Monks and the secular Clerics." ("A *History of Printing*"— Oswald.)

To Friar Lucas Bartholomew Pacioli is due our present-day system of double-entry bookkeeping. His treatise on this subject, published in 1494, was considered important enough to be printed only a quarter of a century after Gutenberg's great invention. This treatise is the foundation upon which practically all subsequent writings concerning double-entry bookkeeping have been predicated.

It was a thirteenth century English Franciscan, Bartholomaeus Anglicus, who composed the first great encyclopedia of science in the middle ages, called "*De Proprietatibus Rerum*"—"Of the Properties of Things."

That the secular and religious history of Ireland was not entirely lost under the destructive Cromwellian hordes is due to the scholarship of the Franciscan Brother Michael O'Clery (1580-1643) and his companions, known to history as "The Four Masters." With vast patience and erudition, they assembled and copied the ancient vellum manuscripts which contained Irish history from the time of Christ to the seventeenth century.

In the exploration of Africa, two centuries before Stanley and Livingstone, the achievements of Brother Peter Farde, a Belgian Franciscan, are noteworthy. While on his way from Lisbon to the Holy Land in 1686, he was captured and sold into slavery. Regaining his freedom, he traversed vast sections of northern and eastern Africa, crossing jungles and deserts, teaching the Catholic Faith and baptizing hundreds of natives. His thrilling experiences in the Dark Continent, and later while shipwrecked on a desert island in the Atlantic, read like a "Robinson Crusoe."

In sociology two Franciscan Friars, Barnabas of Terni (1474) and the Blessed Bernardine of Feltre (1494), were chiefly instrumental in founding the celebrated *monti di pietà*—charitable loan institutions—along the lines of our modern banks, designed to protect the poor against the usury of the money-lenders.

Along with their missionary work begun in the sixteenth century in the Philippine Islands, the Franciscans compiled grammars, dictionaries, and catechisms in the native dialects. They laid out cities, built bridges, tunnels, and water systems; they taught the Filipinos how to grow cocoa, tobacco, and coffee, and to cultivate the silkworm.

Many are unaware, too, that it was a son of St. Francis, Bishop Mullock, O.F.M., of Newfoundland, who first conceived the idea of laying a trans-Atlantic cable, and showed it to be practicable.

A Franciscan Capuchin, Brother Candidus de Magland, of Savoy, was the inventor of the fountain pen.

When we hear of the great Universities of Oxford and Cambridge and the Sorbonne of Paris, we should not forget, as Gladstone remarked, that their golden age was when the humble Friars sat in their *cathedra*—when Duns Scotus, Alexander of Hales, Adam Marsh, Peckham, and Ockham taught the world.

It is recognized that the tragedy *Adamo Caduto* (The Fallen Adam), written in 1647 by the Franciscan Seraphin della Salandra, supplied the inspiration for Milton's Paradise Lost.

To the Third Order of St. Francis belonged the great

poets Dante, Tasso, and Petrarch. Columbus, too, was a follower of St. Francis, as were the great composers Palestrina and Gounod. Galvani, the discoverer of galvanism; Volta and Galileo, the scientists; the painters and sculptors, Cimabue, Giotto, Michelangelo, Raphael, Murillo, and Leonardo da Vinci were Tertiaries of St. Francis. Raymond Lullus, the Spanish philosopher; Sir Thomas More, England's great Chancellor; Vasco da Gama, the navigator; Lope da Vega and Calderon, the authors; and Frederic Ozanam, the founder of the St. Vincent de Paul Society, all were members of the Third Order of St. Francis. These are only a few of the many, and yet what an illustrious array do they present—men of science, of art, of literature, and greater than all, men of piety!

It would be difficult to enumerate the members of royalty who have worn the habit of St. Francis. Preeminent among royal Tertiaries are St. Louis IX, King of France; St. Elizabeth, Queen of Portugal; St. Elizabeth of Hungary; and St. Ferdinand, King of Spain.

"Even those who care little about the Order he [St. Francis] founded, and who have scant sympathy for the Church to which he belonged, find themselves looking across the ages for his guidance and invoking his name in grateful remembrance." (*Report of the Florida Historical Society.*)

The Franciscans and the Church

"Go ye into the whole world, and preach the Gospel."
(St. Mark xvi, 15.)

AFTER the death of St. Francis, his followers journeyed to all parts of the known world, adhering faithfully to the spirit with which he had inspired them, and continuing their mission with unremitting zeal. This new soldiery which God had given to the Church was destined to revive the spirit of Jesus Christ among the nations, while it bore to distant lands the Cross of Christ and the banner of civilization.

The Order of St. Francis has carried on at all times the work of preaching in Catholic lands, and the work of missions among the heathen. Volumes might be

[135]

written of the labors, the sufferings, and the triumphs of the Franciscan missionaries; no Order in the Church has surpassed them in zeal for the propagation of the Gospel. St. Francis himself visited the Holy Land; later he sent five Friars to Morocco, where all were martyred. Franciscans preached in Tartary about the middle of the thirteenth century, and in China and Armenia before the end of it. So great was their influence in Armenia that King Haytion II renounced his throne and became a member of the Order, in which, as Brother John, he died in 1300.

Pope Gregory IX about 1230 officially committed to the Franciscans the care of the Holy Places of Palestine. This charge was confirmed by Clement VI in 1342, and again by Benedict XV in 1919. This duty they still discharge, regarding the Holy Land as "The Pearl of the Franciscan Missions."

A Franciscan missionary, John of Monte Corvino, Archbishop of Peking, about 1305 translated the New Testament and the Psalms into the Chinese language, in addition to which work, he built numerous churches in that country.

Franciscans were established in Bosnia in 1340, in Bulgaria about 1366, and in Caucasia in 1370. We find them taking a large share in the conversion of the natives of the Canary Islands in and after 1423. In the fourteenth century the Franciscans were already evangelizing Morocco, Tunis, Libya, Egypt, and Abyssinia, in Africa; it was a Franciscan Archbishop, John of Albuquerque, who welcomed the great St. Francis Xavier to India. About 1490 they established a mission in the Congo, which bore great fruit, and before 1600 the Sons of St. Francis were spreading the Gospel in the Kingdom of Japan, where many gave their lives as martyrs.

Left: IN THE MONASTERY GARDEN
ALVERNA CHAPEL; SACRED HEART STATUE; ST. PASCHAL CHAPEL

Imitating St. Francis, the Friars unselfishly served the lepers, of which work one historian remarks that it was "perhaps the only activity where envy did not pursue them." During the Black Death in the Middle Ages some 20,000 Franciscans, or one-third of the Order at that time, fell victims to their care of the plague-stricken.

During the century following the Protestant Reformation in 1520, more than 500 Franciscans were martyred for the Catholic Faith in Germany, England, Holland, and other European countries.

There is no savage nation which the Franciscan missionaries have not sought to evangelize; no land so distant or shore so unknown that they have not watered it with the sweat of their brows, and often with their blood. In our day their apostolic zeal has not abated, and their missions are spread to all parts of the globe. The disciples of St. Francis are found in Asia, under the burning sun of Africa, in antipodal Australia, in the vast regions of North and South America, and among the savage tribes of the islands of the South Seas.

Truly can it be said that the spirit of St. Francis has pervaded the whole Church, for, besides the three great branches of the Franciscan Order: the Friars Minor, the Minor Conventuals, and the Minor Capuchins, and the numerous Sisterhoods of the Third Order, many Tertiaries of St. Francis, inspired by his ideals, have founded other Religious Orders. Notable among them are:

St. Ignatius, founder of the Jesuits, and his two great followers, St. Francis Xavier, Apostle of India, and St. Francis Borgia;

St. Cajetan, founder of the Theatines;

St. Charles Borromeo, founder of the Oblates;

St. Vincent de Paul, founder of the Lazarists and of the Sisters of Charity;

St. Philip Neri, founder of the Oratorians;

St. Camillus of Lellis, founder of the Servants of the Sick;

St. Francis de Sales and St. Jane Frances de Chantal, founders of the Sisters of the Visitation;

St. Paul of the Cross, founder of the Passionists;

St. Alphonsus Liguori, founder of the Redemptorists;

St. Angela, founder of the Ursulines;

St. John Baptist de la Salle, founder of the Christian Brothers;

St. John Bosco, founder of the Salesians;

Father Olier, founder of the Sulpicians.

Five Franciscans have occupied the See of St. Peter as Visible Head of Christ's Church, namely: Pope Nicholas IV (1288-1292); Alexander V (1409-1410); Sixtus IV (Conventual Friar, 1471-1484); Sixtus V (Conventual, 1585-1590); and Clement XIV (Conventual, 1769-1774).

Pius IX, Leo XIII, Pius X, Benedict XV and Pius XI, and numerous other Popes, as members of the Third Order, have been proud to call themselves sons of St. Francis. Many Cardinals have been members of

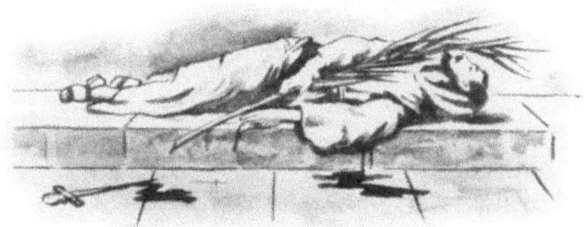

the Third Order, as well as a multitude of Archbishops and Bishops throughout the world.

Not only has the Franciscan Order throughout the centuries of its existence given God and His Church great Saints in the past, but today, among those recently elevated to the honors of the Altar, are numbered the spiritual children of St. Francis. Many of them have given their lives in testimony of their faith, both in the Old World and in the New, where in recent years and on our own continent, our confrères have shed their blood for Christ in neighboring Mexico.

The Franciscans and America

"Blessed is he that cometh in the name of the Lord."
(Psalm cxvii, 26.)

THE Franciscans were instrumental in the discovery of America. Father Juan Perez, Superior of the Monastery at Rabida in Spain, himself a learned cosmographer, entered warmly into the designs of Columbus, who in turn was confirmed in his belief of the earth's sphericity by the writings of the Franciscan Roger Bacon. Father Perez used his influence with Queen Isabella, whose Chaplain he had been, to persuade her to equip the memorable expedition of 1492. In the following year, Father Juan Perez himself came to America with Columbus' second voyage. He established the first Christian Church in the New World at a small settlement on the island of Haiti, and was the celebrant of the first Mass offered up under western skies. His image, together with those of Pope Alexander and other prelates connected with the discovery of America, may be seen on the magnificent bronze doors of the Capitol in Washington. It is of particular interest that Columbus petitioned the Spanish Sovereigns to give to the Holy Land a portion of such revenues as might be derived from the discovery of America.

In 1673 English Franciscans were engaged in missionary work in Maryland, where they were preceded three years before by the Irish Franciscan Recollects, Father Hobart, one of their number, dying there a martyr of charity. In Pennsylvania, Father Hadock was subjected to severe persecution for having celebrated Mass publicly, and during the War of Independence Father Seraphin Bandal preached frequently before the members of the American Congress.

The first printing press in North America was set up and operated by the Franciscans in Mexico. On the bronze doors of the new Rare Book Division of the Library of Congress is the ecclesiastical coat-of-arms which appeared on the title page of the first book printed in the New World, the "*Doctrina Breve,*" published in Mexico in 1539, under the auspices of the Franciscan Bishop Juan de Zumárraga.

The first recorded mention of petroleum oil in the United States was made in 1627 by a Franciscan, Father Joseph de la Roche d'Aillon, who penetrated into what is now the State of New York, in the vicinity of Lake Erie, in 1626.

There were early Franciscan missions in Brazil and Peru. The Friars Minor were welcomed to Mexico by

Cortez in 1523, and under their holy leader, Martin de Valenza, they planted Christianity in that empire, whence they went forth to preach the Gospel in New Mexico (1539), in Arizona, in Texas (1600), and lastly, in California (1769). The numerous Franciscan Missions in the south-west were appropriately named by contemporary writers: "The Kingdom of St. Francis."

In tribute to the memory of the famous Padre Junipero Serra, the State of California erected a magnificent bronze statue, representing the Friar in his Franciscan habit, in the United States Capitol. The great pioneer work carried on by Father Serra and his fellow-Franciscans in the exploration and development of California was truly remarkable. So indelible has been the impress of their efforts, through the foundation of the famous Franciscan Missions, that some one has said that the names of the cities in a California railroad time-table are like the Litany of the Saints. Between the years 1769 and 1854, the 144 Friars laboring in California's famous Missions converted about 80,000 Indians, their unselfish work among the aborigines "filling one of the brightest pages of Franciscan history."

The Venerable Antonio Margil, who established the missions in Texas, was the first person from the United States proposed for canonization. Nearly half a century was spent by the zealous missionary among the Indians of Central and North America.

In their apostolic labors in South America, the Friars often had to defend their converts against the exploitation of the invaders, and in Mexico a striking feature of early Franciscan activity was the education of children, despite great opposition. The Franciscans were the first to introduce compulsory education into the New World. One may gain an idea of the difficulties which beset this innovation from the fact that many wealthy families, in opposition to it, sent their servants to the schools instead of their children.

The first missionary work in Mexico was carried on by three Flemish Franciscans, who arrived there in 1523. One of these pioneers, Brother Pedro de Gante, established a great school, attended by over a thousand Mexican boys, who there received instruction in the elementary and higher branches, and the mechanical and fine arts. Brother Pedro found time amid his labors to translate the Church's hymns into the Aztec language, and in 1555 Father Alonzo de Molina, a former pupil of the Friars, published a Mexican-Spanish dictionary, which is still regarded as standard. The founding of the first high school and the first free boarding schools on the American continent are among the immortal accomplishments of the Franciscans in Mexico. Writing of Spanish-American education, a former Yale professor says: "Provisions were made for its promotion on a far greater scale than was possible or even attempted in the English colonies. The early Franciscan missionaries built a school beside each church."

Toward the end of 1577, the Franciscans began the

evangelization of Florida, which then embraced all that territory extending "northward to the pole and westward to the Pacific Ocean." It was one of these missionaries who wrote the first book ever published in an Indian language, an "Abridgment of Christian Doctrine." By 1646 the Franciscan missions existed in 44 settlements scattered from St. Augustine to Chesapeake Bay. What is believed to be the oldest building in the United States is the Franciscan Monastery in St. Augustine, Florida, built about 1600, and now known as "St. Francis Barracks."

The Franciscans were not only the first missionaries in those portions of North America and the islands settled by the Spaniards, but also in the Northern regions along the Atlantic coast, explored by Cabot under the auspices of England. Years before the Pilgrims anchored in Cape Cod, the intrepid Franciscan LeCaron had penetrated the land of the Mohawk and evangelized the Huron.

The first exploration of the Great Lakes was made by the "Stanley of North America," the Franciscan Father Hennepin. He named Niagara Falls in honor of St. Anthony, a name once borne also by the majestic Hudson river, and he was the first to explore the Mississippi from source to mouth. The Franciscan John of Torres was with De Soto when he discovered the "Father of Waters."

The first Christian Martyr in the New World was a Franciscan, Father Garcia de Padilla, who was slain for the Faith in what is now the State of Nebraska.

The first Bishop in what is now the United States was Father Juan Zuarez, a member of the Franciscan Order, and Father Michael Egan, a Franciscan, was the first Bishop of Philadelphia, being appointed to that See in 1810.

Basilica of the Agony in Gethsemane

The Franciscans and the Holy Land

"Upon thy walls, O Jerusalem, I have appointed watchmen." (Isaias lxii, 6.)

THE presence of the Franciscans in the Holy Land, "the spiritual Motherland of every Christian soul," dates back to 1219. In that year their founder, St. Francis, left some of his disciples in Palestine as the successors of the Crusaders, establishing there a Province of the Order which is still called the Custody of the Holy Land. During the intervening seven centuries, about three thousand Friars sacrificed their lives in times of persecution, while some six thousand died as martyrs of charity during plague and pestilence. But their thinning ranks have always been filled by new volunteers, coming from every country and Province of the Order.

They have been well called "the weak, but invincible army which alone remained to guard the Holy Sepulchre, when kings had abandoned it."

Among the army of martyrs of the Holy Land during the centuries of Turkish régime, may be mentioned those of recent years in Damascus and Armenia, upon some of whom the Church has bestowed the honors of Beatification.

The Custody of the Holy Land comprises not only Palestine, but also Syria, Asia Minor, Lower Egypt and Cyprus. At the present time, some 500 Franciscans of the Holy Land have in their care more than one hundred thousand people, distributed among twelve races. The Friars maintain numerous Sanctuaries, Parishes, Mission Churches and Chapels, besides three orphanages sheltering hundreds of native children. They also conduct colleges, trade and elementary schools, which are attended by more than 4,000 pupils. Indeed, long before the advent of the British mandatory power, the Franciscans established schools among the under-privileged natives wherever possible to do so. Their educational activities in the Holy Land, of necessity often hidden from the Turkish officials, took definite shape in 1632, by direction of the Holy See. So extensive was this work of the Friars that it was said that almost all Arabs living within their jurisdiction owed whatever education they possessed to the "Brothers of the Cord," as they are called by them. The Franciscans, moreover, provide numerous houses for the shelter of poor families, and help to support thousands of destitute persons. In addition to these institutions, they have hospices for pilgrims, established by order of the Holy See in various cities of the Holy Land, where a cordial welcome is extended to all, regardless of creed or nationality.

As early as 1352 the Franciscans erected in Jerusalem their first public hospital, at a time when even the idea was new to Europe. Thus the Friars have exercised their ministry of charity ever since their establishment in Palestine, and they have been guides and protectors to countless pilgrims who have flocked there during the centuries.

In 1846 the Franciscans established in Jerusalem a printing office, today considered the best in Palestine, publishing works in Arabic, Turkish, Armenian, Greek, Hebrew, Latin, and all modern languages. In connection with the principal Monastery of St. Saviour in Jerusalem, there is a large and important library, frequented by students of various nationalities and creeds.

The saintly Louis DeGoesbriand, first Bishop of Burlington, Vermont, on returning from a Pilgrimage to the Holy Land in 1879, wrote: "The Popes have appointed the Franciscans guardians of the Holy Sepulchre and of all the Holy Places in the Holy Land. For upwards of six hundred years these devoted Religious have kept watch over the Tomb of Our Lord at Jerusalem, over the Grotto of Bethlehem, over the holy dwelling at Nazareth, and many other places. During those six hundred and fifty years, hundreds of them were put to death for the Faith, but others came in the place of those who were slain. The children of St. Francis remain true to their duty. . . . I will add for the honor of the humble sons of St. Francis, that were it not for their presence in the Holy Land, all the Holy Places which we so justly venerate would have long since been occupied and desecrated by the schismatics, the Jews, or the Mohammedans."

Devotions Founded by the Franciscans

"In the churches I will bless Thee, O Lord."
(Psalm xxv, 12.)

MANY of the greatest and most popular devotions of the Church owe their origin to the Sons of St. Francis. Principal among them may be mentioned:

The beautiful custom of the Christmas Crib, originated in 1223 at Greccio, in Italy, by St. Francis himself.

The recitation of the *Angelus* morning, noon, and night, in memory of Our Lord's Incarnation, was established by the Franciscans, as was the tolling the church bell at nightfall to remind the faithful to pray for the dead.

To the great intellect and earnest efforts of Friar John Duns Scotus (1265–1308) must be attributed the wide adoption of a Feast in honor of the Immaculate Conception. This dogma, solemnly promulgated in 1854 by Pope Pius IX, teaches that Mary was ever preserved by the merits of Christ from all stain of original sin, that she might more worthily fulfill the exalted dignity of becoming the Mother of Christ the Lord, for which God had chosen her from all eternity.

The Forty Hours' Devotion in honor of the Blessed Sacrament was instituted in 1537 by the Friars, and Perpetual Adoration of the Blessed Sacrament was established by the Franciscans in Milan.

The popular devotion of the Way of the Cross was introduced by the Franciscans into their churches, and Pope Clement XII extended this devotion to the uni-

St. Francis' Christmas Crib

versal Church, reserving to the Order of St. Francis the right to bless the Stations of the Cross.

The great Franciscan Missionaries, Saints Bernardine of Siena, James of the Marches, and John Capistran, spread the devotion to the Holy Name of Jesus, under which banner hundreds of thousands of Catholic men of the United States are enrolled. It was St. Bernardine, too, who popularized the Greek IHS monogram of the Name of Jesus (IHΣOΥΣ).

About the year 1279, Pope Nicholas III adopted the Franciscan Breviary for the use of the Churches in Rome.

The following ecclesiastical festivals were established through the Order of St. Francis:

January 1, The Holy Name, approved by Pope Clement VII, 1530;

March 19, St. Joseph, observed as early as 1399;

February 24, St. Gabriel the Archangel, established 1541;

Sunday after Pentecost, Feast of the Most Holy Trinity;

July 2, The Visitation, ordered in 1263;

July 26, St. Anne, in the same year;

August 2, Portiuncula Indulgence, 1216;

August 6, The Transfiguration, prescribed in 1458;

August 16, St. Joachim, Father of the Blessed Virgin, observed in 1505;

October 2, The Guardian Angels, observed in 1500;

December 8, The Immaculate Conception, observed as early as 1263.

Among the liturgical prayers originated by the Franciscans are enumerated:

The hymn *Veni Sancte Spiritus* in honor of the Holy Ghost, attributed to St. Bonaventure;

The *Stabat Mater*, by Fra Jacopone da Todi;

THROUGH THE ARCHES OF ROSARY PORTICO

The *Dies Irae*, written by Fra Thomas of Celano;

The concluding words, "Now and at the hour of our death," of the *Hail Mary*, came into popular usage through the Franciscan Order;

St. Bernardine of Siena composed the prayer "*Sub tuum praesidium*—We fly to thy patronage";

To Bl. Bernardine of Feltre, who died in 1494, is authoritatively ascribed the authorship of the beautiful Communion prayer "*Anima Christi*—Soul of Christ, sanctify me";

Pope Sixtus V, a Franciscan, introduced the recitation of the familiar prayer "Blessed be God."

THE CLOISTER GARTH

The Religious Life

"Behold how good and how pleasant it is for brethren to dwell together in unity." (Psalm cxxxii, 1.)

RELIGIOUS life is founded deeply in the Gospel and is its most beautiful flower. Even in the Old Testament we find the Nazarites, who consecrated themselves to God by vows. Josephus speaks of these Essenes, whose life was almost similar to that of the Benedictines of our era.

From the beginning of Christianity, many renounced the pleasures of the world to follow the Saviour more closely. The deserts became populated with hermits, who later consolidated into communities. Thus were founded the Orders of St. Antony of Egypt and of St. Basil.

With Christianity, the monastic spirit spread to the West also. St. Benedict, the great Patriarch of western monasticism, erected his monasteries upon the débris of the Roman Empire. Lord Macaulay, writing of the beneficial influence of the monastic institutions, says: "Had not such retreats been scattered here and there among the huts of a miserable peasantry and the castles of a ferocious aristocracy, European society would have consisted merely of beasts of burden and beasts of prey."

The monasteries were beacons of light amidst the darkness and tempest of the great migration of nations toward a new Christian civilization. "It was there," writes the author of "Legends of the Monastic Orders," "that learning trimmed her lamps, there contemplation plumed her wings, there the traditions of art, preserved from age to age by lonely, studious men, kept alive in form and color the idea of a beauty beyond that of earth, of a might beyond that of the spear and the shield, of a divine sympathy with suffering humanity."

Apace with Christian civilization, new Orders sprang up in the Church of God, each adapted to a special need in the Church. Among the illustrious founders none is known better than St. Francis, the Poor Man of Assisi. His Rule is the strictest enforcement of the evangelical virtues, and its chief characteristic is simplicity and poverty.

The Franciscans soon numbered thousands, and Cardinal Vaughan has admirably pictured their activities in the following beautiful words: "We find the same Friars who nursed the lepers, who preached from the village crosses, who cheered the laborers in the harvest fields, or the traveler by the wayside, who helped the sick, the sorrowful, and the sinful in the slums of our mediaeval cities, who amused and instructed the multitudes by their miracle plays, are the same Brotherhood who filled with distinction the professorial chairs at Oxford, and so took the lead in the very van of theological learning, as to make our English Universities the envy of Europe."

The work of the Monks and Friars was a noble one, and

monasticism still exercises a singular fascination upon the minds of today. Dr. Johnson, staunchest of Protestants, tells us that "he never thought of a monastery but in imagination he kissed its stones."

The monastery is to the outer world a sort of mysterious institution. It is in fact a commonwealth, founded on the principles of the early Christians. There no one possesses anything of his own; there the day is divided between prayer and work; there the practice of the evangelical precepts and counsels is strictly enforced. Every action has a higher motive; the peace of the soul is not disturbed by human cares.

"It is difficult to appreciate in our day the full significance of these old monastic ruins which dot the surface of every European country and some sections of our own. To every mind they suggest at once the life of self-denial and consecration to God which is characteristic of the religious state. But to their contemporaries they had many other offices besides that of homes of penance and prayer and devout meditation. For centuries every monastery answered at one and the same time the purposes of a college, a seminary, a public school, a printing and publishing house, an almshouse, a savings bank and public store house, an industrial commune, an authors' and artists' guild, a school of art and agriculture and handicraft, an inn, a hospital, and doubtless others still. And many of these functions it fulfilled better than any of our modern substitutes even attempt to do." ("*Famous Churches of the World*"—*Washington Star*.)

www.ingramcontent.com/pod-product-compliance
Lightning Source LLC
LaVergne TN
LVHW091259080426
835510LV00007B/326